CW00430639

WHEN YOU PRAY

Lifeway Press®
Brentwood, Tennessee

Published by Lifeway Press® • ©2023 Kelly Minter, Jackie Hill Perry,
Jen Wilkin, Jennifer Rothschild, Jada Edwards, Kristi McLelland
Reprinted September 2023

ISBN: 978-1-0877-6349-1 • Item: 005837641

Dewey decimal classification: 248.3

Subject heading: PRAYER \ PRAYERS \ MEDITATIONS

To order additional copies of this resource, write Lifeway Resources
Customer Service; 200 Powell Place, Suite 100, Brentwood, TN 37027-
7707; FAX order to 615.251.5933; call toll-free 800.458.2772; email
orderentry@lifeway.com; or order online at lifeway.com.

Printed in the United States of America

Lifeway Women Bible Studies,
Lifeway Resources,
200 Powell Place, Suite 100
Brentwood, TN 37027-7707

**EDITORIAL TEAM,
LIFEWAY WOMEN
BIBLE STUDIES**

Becky Loyd
Director,
Lifeway Women

Tina Boesch
Manager

Chelsea Waack
Production Leader

Laura Magness
Content Editor

Erin Franklin
Production Editor

Lauren Ervin
Graphic Designer

Contents

ABOUT THE *Authors*

KELLY MINTER is a Bible teacher and author of numerous Bible studies, including *Encountering God: Cultivating Habits of Faith through the Spiritual Disciplines* and *Ruth: Loss, Love & Legacy*. Along with her love of Scripture, she has great affection for the local church and is privileged to minister to the vulnerable and forgotten with Justice & Mercy International. Currently pursuing an MA in biblical and theological studies at Denver Seminary, Kelly lives in Nashville and is an adoring aunt, flower and vegetable grower, and unfancy cook.

JACKIE HILL PERRY is a Bible teacher, writer, and artist. She is the author of *Jude: Contending for the Faith in Today's Culture*; *Gay Girl, Good God: The Story of Who I Was, and Who God Has Always Been*; and *Holier Than Thou: How God's Holiness Helps Us Trust Him*. At home she is known as wife to Preston and mommy to Eden, Autumn, Sage, and August.

JEN WILKIN is an author and Bible teacher from Dallas, Texas. She has organized and led studies for women in home, church, and parachurch contexts. Her passion is to see others become articulate and committed followers of Christ, with a clear understanding of why they believe what they believe, grounded in the Word of God. Jen is the author of *Ten Words to Live By: Delighting in and Doing What God Commands*; *Women of the Word*; *None Like Him*; *In His Image*; and Bible studies exploring the Sermon on the Mount and the books of Genesis, Exodus, Hebrews, 1 Peter, and 1, 2, 3 John. You can find her at jenwilkin.net.

JENNIFER ROTHSCHILD is the author of nineteen books and Bible studies, including her latest, *Amos: An Invitation to the Good Life*. She's the founder and featured Bible teacher of Fresh Grounded Faith women's events, and she also hosts the *4:13 Podcast* where she shares practical encouragement and biblical wisdom to equip women to live the "I can" life of Philippians 4:13. She's a boy mom, an obsessive audiobook listener, a C. S. Lewis junkie, and a dark chocolate lover! Jennifer has been blind since age fifteen, and she lives every day with confidence and joy knowing that earth is short, and heaven is long. She lives in Springfield, Missouri, with her very own Dr. Phil and their diva dog, Lucy.

JADA EDWARDS is a Bible teacher and discipler. She has committed her life to equipping women of all ages, at all stages, with practical, biblical truth to help them live authentic and transparent lives. Jada is the author of several books, including *The Captive Mind; Be Bold;* and *Thirst*, and she is a contributing author to *World on Fire*. She and her husband Conway planted One Community Church in 2008, where she currently serves as the creative services director and women's director. Jada and Conway are parents to Joah and Chloe, and they live in Allen, Texas.

KRISTI MCLELLAND is a speaker, teacher, writer, and college professor. She has dedicated her life to discipleship, to teaching people how to study the Bible for themselves, and to writing about how God is better than we ever knew by explaining the Bible through a Middle Eastern lens. Kristi is the author of the Bible studies *Jesus and Women: In the First Century and Now* and *The Gospel on the Ground: The Grit and Glory of the Early Church in Acts*. She also hosts the K-LOVE podcast *Pearls* with AccessMore. Kristi regularly leads biblical study trips to Israel, Turkey, Greece, and Italy. For more information about Kristi and what she's up to, visit: newlensbiblicalstudies.com.

ABOUT THIS  Study

This Bible study is unique.

Each session was written by a different Lifeway Women Bible study author.

Each session has video teaching, filmed at a two-day Lifeway Women Live event.

Each author brings her particular style and pacing to the video teaching and personal study. Their individual styles and approaches to study combine to make this a Bible study experience that will open up the words of Scripture to you in a brand new way.

Each day of study begins and ends with guided prayers and prayer prompts to help you build conversation with God into your daily rhythms. The opening prayers to each day are David's words to the Lord from Psalm 119 that capture his delight in God's Word and encourage you to do the same. The closing prayers challenge you to apply what you learned in that day's study.

Because this study is unique, you can use it in different ways.

- Conduct the study as a regular consecutive-week study on your own or with a small group.

- Use this study as a retreat curriculum or large group study, paired with the *When You Pray* Group Experience Kit.

Regardless of how you choose to study, we recommend you check out all the extra resources available at lifeway.com/whenyoupray.

LEADING A GROUP? **A free leader guide PDF** is available for download at lifeway.com/whenyoupray. The leader guide offers several tips and helps, along with discussion guides for each week.

lifeway.com/whenyoupray

WHAT'S *Inside*

PERSONAL STUDY: Each week, you'll have five days of personal study with questions to help you process and apply what you read. After you finish a session of personal study, it's time to watch the teaching video.

WATCH: These pages provide a place to take notes from the video teachings. You'll want to begin your study with the Session One video and then watch the rest of the videos after you finish each session of personal study.

VIDEO ACCESS: With the purchase of this book, you have access to teaching videos that provide content to help you better understand and apply what you just studied in the previous session. **You'll find detailed information for how to access the teaching videos on the card inserted in the back of your Bible study book.**

A NOTE ABOUT BIBLE TRANSLATIONS

This study will primarily use the Christian Standard Bible translation (CSB). However, reading the same passage of Scripture from more than one translation is a helpful study tool, and we'll incorporate several translations in the pages of this book and in the videos. Here are a few of the others we'll use, which will be marked by their abbreviations:

> English Standard Version (ESV)
> New American Standard Bible (NASB)
> New International Version (NIV)
> New King James Version (NKJV)
> New Living Translation (NLT)

You can find all of these translations on a Bible app or websites such as biblegateway.com or biblehub.com.

LOOKING FOR MORE?

You'll find videos from the authors, a free leader guide, promotional resources, and more at **lifeway.com/whenyoupray**

When You Pray

INTRODUCTION

Prayer, simply put, is talking with God. It is designed by God to be a beautiful gift of communication between the Creator and the children created in His image. We are a world of born communicators, so prayer should come naturally to us. But depending on the amount of time you've spent as a follower of Christ, your prayer life has likely ebbed and flowed through seasons of intimate conversation to uncomfortable silence and back again.

Oftentimes, we find it difficult to pray consistently, or we feel like our prayers lack passion and power. Sometimes, we make it to the end of busy days only to realize we haven't prayed at all. In other moments, we're so overcome with longing or loss that we struggle to find words to express the groanings of our hearts. And in other moments, our souls overflow with gratitude for God's grace.

At one point in the Gospel of Luke, we read Jesus "was praying in a certain place, and when he finished, one of his disciples said to him, 'Lord, teach us to pray'" (Luke 11:1). Of all the conversations the four Gospels give us between Jesus and His disciples, this was the only time when one of them asked Jesus to teach him how to do something. It seems he knew what you know: Prayer is important, and it's hard. He also knew Jesus was the right One to ask. Anytime the disciples were looking for Him, they found Him in prayer.

Thankfully, just as Jesus taught His disciples to pray, God's Word gives us invaluable insight on this topic, too. Most notably, we learn there's no one right way! Some prayers are deeply personal; others are intended for a gathered group. Some are carefully composed; others are spontaneous. Some prayers are cries of longing and frustration; other prayers are songs of praise. Some are confessions of personal sin; others are intercession on behalf of another. And each of them—every single prayer we utter—is a means of positioning ourselves to hear from God and know Him more.

As the prayers of the Bible demonstrate, God invites all your words, all the time. But as you study the prayers of the Bible and adopt their rhythms as your own, you'll learn that prayer is about so much more than asking God for things. It's about a never-ending conversation with your heavenly Father.

GOD INVITES ALL YOUR WORDS, ALL THE TIME.

Throughout God's Word, we encounter many voices whose prayers model the act of prayer for us. In this study we'll consider six of them—Jesus's model prayer (His response when the disciples asked Him to teach them) and examples of petition, praise, lament, intercession, and unity. To help, we've assembled a group of beloved Bible teachers who will unpack the meaning of these prayers. Through each of their unique writing styles, Bible study methods, and teaching gifts, these women bring their God-given wisdom to the prayers of the Bible and will help you learn what to say when you pray.

Laura Magness

WATCH
SESSION ONE

Watch the Session One video and take notes below.

TO ACCESS THE VIDEO SESSIONS, USE THE INSTRUCTIONS
IN THE BACK OF YOUR BIBLE STUDY BOOK.

Discuss

If you are part of a *When You Pray* Bible study group, use this page to take notes during your group time and to keep a record of prayer requests that are mentioned.

Your Kingdom Come

BY KELLY MINTER

Prayer is one of those incredibly significant parts of our Christian lives that's also attended by challenges, questions, and mysteries. It's not always as easy or straightforward of a practice as we wish it to be. Perhaps you find yourself wondering, among many other things, *Am I praying the "right way," according to God's will?* I think Jesus's disciples wanted to know this, too. What could give us more assurance about the practice of prayer than praying the very words of Jesus? This is why I'm eager to begin our study on prayer together with the words Jesus taught His followers to pray.

The Lord's Prayer, which we find versions of in Matthew 6:9-13 and Luke 11:2-4, will set the foundation for the rest of our study and all our prayers. This is essential because we don't want to just study prayer—we want to become deeper and more effective pray-ers. I suppose this is a good time for me to confess that prayer has historically been a weakness of mine; it's a discipline I've had to grow in. The prayer of Jesus we're studying this week has been especially helpful for me because when I don't know what to pray, it puts words to my longings. When I'm distracted, it keeps me on track with its praises and petitions. When I'm confused, it helps me pray according to God's will. And as much as it's a model prayer, we shouldn't think of it as a rote one. Each portion of Jesus's prayer allows for a thousand others to be uttered, prayers that are specific to our own lives and His work in our world.

As we begin this first week of study, it's helpful to keep in mind the context of the Lord's Prayer. It sits at the dead center of the Sermon on the Mount, Jesus's teaching on how to live as a citizen of the kingdom of heaven right here in our everyday lives. Surely this is no coincidence—prayer is central to Jesus's teaching. Since Jesus's Sermon shines light on the prayer we're studying, we'll turn to different portions of it throughout the week.

What a joy we have ahead of us. May Jesus Himself teach us to pray.

This Week's Prayer

BIBLE PASSAGE
Matthew 6:5-13

PRAYER TYPE
The Lord's Prayer

*Our Father in heaven,
your name be
honored as holy.
Your kingdom come.
Your will be done
on earth as it is
in heaven.*

MATTHEW 6:9b-10

DAY ONE
THE SECRET PLACE

Before we get to this week's main passage of study, TURN TO LUKE'S GOSPEL AND READ 11:1-4.

What did the disciple ask Jesus to do?

As obvious as this may seem, what do we learn about prayer from the fact that the disciples felt they needed to be taught how to pray?

The more Jesus's disciples understood He was moving them from an Old Testament perspective of covenants and laws to what life would look like in relationship with Him, the more they realized He was forming a distinct community out of them. The disciples wanted to know how to pray as that new community in light of His kingdom having come.[1] And as followers of Christ today, so do we.

To better understand "The Lord's Prayer"—some call it "The Disciple's Prayer," since we're the ones praying it—we'll begin where Jesus did. He did not actually jump straight into praying; rather, He focused on our approach to prayer and the nature of our heavenly Father to whom we pray.

READ MATTHEW 6:5-8.

Sometimes the best way to learn how to do something is by first learning how *not* to do it. When my dad was teaching me how to drive in our family's 4-cylinder, stick-shift minivan (the worst vehicle to cut your driving teeth on), he would say, or occasionally yell, things like, *Don't let your foot off the clutch too fast. Don't roll back into the car behind you on an incline at a light. Don't run yellow lights. Kelly, you're stalling!* I had a running list in the *Whatever-You-Do-Don't-Do-This* category. Under much less stressful conditions, Jesus employed this helpful technique when it comes to prayer.

Before you begin today's study, pray **Psalm 119:18,**

Open my eyes so that I may contemplate wondrous things from your instruction.

In verse 5, Jesus told His disciples not to pray like what type of people? Why?

Whether we pray to be noticed or don't pray so we aren't noticed, both have to do with fear of people instead of a reverence for God.

In first-century Jewish culture, the Jews prayed three times a day—in the morning, around mid-afternoon, and before bed. Some of the religious leaders timed their arrival to sacred places like the temple or crowded places like the street corners so people could take notice of their spiritual dedication. Their motive had more to do with being applauded by people than meeting with God. Jesus said, *Don't pray like this.*

I can't help but wonder if Jesus were giving this message today, would He take an opposite approach by encouraging us *to* pray in front of people more than we do? Not only are most of us not guilty of praying on street corners, we may not want to thank God for our meal in a restaurant or ask a neighbor if we can stop to pray for her in a challenging season for fear of what people might think. Whether we pray to be noticed or don't pray so we aren't noticed, both have to do with fear of people instead of a reverence for God.

In what settings do you feel the pull to pray in a way that others will notice how spiritual you are? Why do you think this is a temptation?

In what settings do you avoid praying because of what others might think of you? What do you think is your root fear?

LOOK BACK AT VERSE 6. What three things did Jesus tell us we should do when we pray?

1.

2.

3.

Jesus wasn't suggesting we never pray in public or with other people. The very nature of the Disciple's Prayer is one that's to be prayed in community, not to mention we see the disciples praying together at various times in the New Testament (see Luke 9:28; 22:45-46; Acts 1:14; 2:42; 12:12). Jesus's focus is on the motivation of our hearts. If we escape to a private room where no one can see us and close the door so no one can hear us, our prayers become solely about meeting with God rather than about what we might gain from others.

When we pray *to* commune with the living God, Jesus said our Father *sees* us in secret. Whereas the religious hypocrites prayed loudly to be seen by people, the praying woman who closes the door in her home does so to be seen by God. And He not only *sees* her in secret; He "*is* in secret" (v. 6, emphasis mine), meaning He dwells with us in our quiet places, a reference to His omnipresence (He is present everywhere) but also to His genuine nature.[2] Our heavenly Father doesn't feed off flashy and showy displays of religiosity; rather, He delights to show up in the quiet places for those seeking authentic communion with Him. What an invitation of intimacy prayer is.

> **Our heavenly Father doesn't feed off flashy and showy displays of religiosity; rather, He delights to show up in the quiet places for those seeking authentic communion with Him.**

> How does the Father seeing what no one else sees and being uniquely present with you in a way no one else can encourage you to spend time with Him in prayer?

Jesus used the word *reward* in both verses 5 and 6.

> Describe the hypocrites' reward.

> Who rewards the person who prays with the right motives?

The reward the hypocrites were after was the reward they got—the finicky and unsatisfying applause of people. I expect Jesus to counteract that by saying genuine prayers don't come with rewards. But He surprises us. Our heavenly Father rewards us when we pray. He doesn't specify the reward but guarantees it. I've had to think about this because it seems counter-intuitive that God would reward us for praying when the whole point of this passage is that we would seek Him with pure motives instead of for, well, rewards.

But when I think about the ways we reward one another, I realize how much of it is based on mutual trust. When I tell my nieces and nephew that if they're kind to each other we'll have Mexican for dinner, at least part of their reason for obeying me is that they believe I'll do what I've said—chips and salsa for all. Similarly, when we forgo the applause of people for the reward of our Father, we're trusting that being with Him will bring greater blessing than what others can bring us. Even if His reward doesn't come as quickly as a congratulatory word from the crowd, we believe He will do as He promised. Looking forward to prayer's reward isn't selfish; it's rooted in trust.

What rewards have you experienced through prayer?

LOOK BACK AT VERSES 7-8. In verse 5, Jesus told His disciples not to pray like the hypocrites. Whom did He tell them not to pray like in verse 7?

How did the Gentiles (pagans) pray?

The term *Gentiles* was another way of referring to pagan people who worshiped a pantheon of gods. Whether they were begging the sun god to bring them heat or the rain god to bring them showers for their crops, their gods were unpredictable. There was no possibility of relationship, only the hope of manipulating the gods to do what they needed them to. So, they carried on with empty repetitions.

What reason did Jesus give for why we don't need to pray like the Gentiles (v. 8)?

The fact that our heavenly Father already knows what we need before we ask Him brings some of us comfort and others frustration. What is your response and why?

I used to wonder why we have to pray if God already knows what we need. But then I thought: *What if our Father in heaven* didn't *know what we needed?* That would really be terrifying. We'd be left babbling for His attention like the Gentiles, scrambling to have our needs met, hoping He heard the urgent prayer we prayed. "If God is worth His salt, He can be nothing less than all-knowing."[3]

How does God's personal, powerful, and all-knowing nature influence the way you pray and the words you use?

We'll look more at God's nature and the relational aspect of prayer in the coming days, but let's close with a reminder of these wonderful truths. First, we don't have to pray like the religious hypocrites because what we long for in prayer isn't receiving accolades from people but a relationship with God. Second, we don't have to pray like the irreligious pagans who carried on in hopes of having their needs met because our God is different. He is loving, personal, all-knowing, and delights to meet with us in the secret place. And lastly, prayer is filled with reward. As we will see in more detail this week, our Father delights to give good things to His children. So whether He rewards us with tangible gifts or shares with us more of His presence, we are blessed when we pray.

When You Pray Today

What a perfect time to find a **"secret place"** so you can pray to your heavenly Father. Remember, He not only *sees* in secret but *is* in secret with you. **Find that quiet place.** Whether it's a favored chair, a park you like to walk in, or your actual closet, **He longs to meet with you.**

Before you begin today's study, pray **Psalm 119:18,**

Open my eyes so that I may contemplate wondrous things from your instruction.

DAY TWO

BEGINNING WITH GOD

I wonder how you begin your prayers. Do you jump straight in? Do you pause in silence before praying? Do you pray Scripture? And with what kinds of things do you start? Jesus teaches us to begin our prayers by focusing on God. This seems like the most obvious thing in the world to me until I realize I don't always start here. How often do I immediately jump into my pressing needs, my unmet longings, and my day's concerns?

This isn't all bad—I believe God desires we bring Him our earnest desires. But the Lord's Prayer makes certain that before we get to any of our personal petitions, we have the privilege of correcting course, bending our wills toward His despite our resistance, clinging to our Father's ways even when leaving behind our own feels like it just might kill us. It is here, at the very top of our prayers, that we place ourselves under the rule and reign of our loving heavenly Father. Here, we align our hearts and ambitions with His! Here, we say, *Your name* above our ego, our being right, our being esteemed by others. Here, we declare *Your ways* above all others because no one is greater, more loving, or more worthy than the Father in heaven who is *ours*.

"When we start with Him, all other petitions are sure to fall in holy line."[4]

> **READ MATHEW 6:9-13, giving special attention to verses 9-10.**

> **Jesus's Model Prayer begins with:**

> Our _____ in _____

In first-century Judaism, it was unusual to refer to God as Father because of the title's intimate nature. Jesus revealed that with the inauguration of His kingdom, God has become "as accessible as the most loving human parent."[5] At the same time, He remains Almighty God. This combination offers the kindness and care of a loving Father with the power and glory of His position in heaven.

You could have a tender father who's without power, and you can have a mighty strong dad who's without love, but reflect for a moment on this: How does having God as both loving Father and heavenly Ruler shape the way you pray?

From verses 9-10, fill in the following:

We want God's _____ to be hallowed or honored as holy.

We want His _____ to come.

We want His _____ to be done.

Each of these petitions is a slight variation of the same request.[6] Like three tributaries running into the same river, our desire for God's renown, reign, and rule all flow toward His throne. As broad as the ideas of God's name, kingdom, and will are, it will help to define them as best we can in a limited space.

GOD'S NAME: A name represents the person who bears it. So, when we exalt God's name as honored and holy, we're exalting His Person, His actions, His nature. God's name isn't merely about His title. It refers to His person, character, and authority.[7]

READ PSALM 30:4. How did the psalmist describe God's name?

Multiple places in the Old Testament describe God's name as holy (see Ps. 97:12; 103:1; 111:9; Isa. 29:23). When we honor God's holy name, we're honoring God.

READ 1 SAMUEL 12:20-25. On what basis did God choose not to reject His people, even though they had sinned against Him (v. 22)?

We see here that God was good and gracious to His people when they didn't deserve it—when they rejected Him for a human king. But we also see that His love and mercy for them was a reflection of His holy name. This unfathomable grace would ultimately reach its fulfillment in a new name.

READ PHILIPPIANS 2:5-11. How does God treat the name of Jesus (v. 9)?

Names have always been important. We name our children after loved ones. We honor those who have passed away by preserving their names on tombstones. We even name companies, ministries, and awards after special people. We do this not because particular names are so great but because we esteem the person who bears the name.

GOD'S KINGDOM: Matthew's Gospel mentions the phrase *kingdom of heaven* thirty-two times.[8] In its simplest description it is God's perfect rule and reign through the person of Jesus. I love how Dallas Willard describes it, "The *kingdom* of God is the range of his *effective* will: that is, it is the domain where what he prefers is actually what happens."[9] I want to live within the realm of God's preferences, don't you? To better understand what the kingdom of heaven (which Matthew often refers to as "the kingdom of God") is, we'll look up some key passages.

Read the following verses about the kingdom of heaven:

Matthew 3:1-2; 4:17	What about the kingdom of heaven caused John the Baptist and Jesus to preach repentance?	
Matthew 4:23	What did Jesus travel around preaching?	
Matthew 6:33	Where is God's kingdom supposed to sit in our daily priorities?	
Matthew 19:13-15	What is the disposition of those who make up the kingdom of heaven?	
Matthew 24:14	How far will the good news of the kingdom reach?	

The kingdom of heaven isn't an easy thing to grasp. "This must surely be why Jesus spoke of it in parables when trying to explain its nature. It's like a mustard seed, He said, yeast working its way through dough, a hidden treasure, a merchant seeking a priceless pearl, a fisherman's net! For all its complexities, it's good to be reminded that one way Jesus described the kingdom is simply that it is *good news*."[10]

GOD'S WILL: The term *God's will* refers to the "redemptive and moral intent of God for this world and for God's people."[11] When we pray for God's will, we're praying for Him to act.[12] We're also agreeing to work in accordance with His purposes so we can be active participants in what He's accomplishing on earth.[13]

I've often said that if not for God's Word the will of God would rarely occur to me. When someone hurts me, my immediate instinct is not to forgive. When my parents need my help because they've forgotten their computer passwords, patience is rarely my first inclination. Before understanding Jesus's teaching on generosity, I loved spending my money on myself. We could go on and on. When we pray for God's will, we're praying according to His Word. Jesus's entire Sermon on the Mount depicts His will, so if you're not sure what His will is in a certain situation, Matthew 5–7 is a wonderful place to go and reflect.

> In what area of your life are you struggling to pray for God's will to be done? Look up that topic in the index of your Bible or do a topical search on your Bible app for a list of related Bible passages. Then, pick one that will help you pray for His will to be done in that area of your life. And when in doubt, simply pray Matthew 6:10.

Praying for God's rule and reign was much harder for me to pray when I was younger. This is at least partially due to the fact that my own will and kingdom are not nearly as enchanting as they once were. My unbridled will has gotten me into some painful situations, and ruling my own kingdom—which is a peaceless existence, a constant looking over my shoulder, a swirl of strife—isn't nearly as much fun as it sounds. This is one reason I find the Lord's Prayer so refreshing. At the very top of the prayer, we get to set the most important things in our lives straight: we want God's name to be glorified, His kingdom to come, and His will to be done, not our own. *We really do!* And if we don't, we pray to want to want it.

Verse 10 in Matthew 6 culminates most remarkably. We want God's

renown and reign to be done on _____ as it is in _____.

Prayer can often seem so lofty that it's detached from our real lives at school, home, or the office. We may not think of God being able to break into our singleness, marriage, parenting, friendships, health, or finances. But think of what Jesus is revealing here: As God's perfect will is being worked in heaven, we are to pray for its inbreaking right here in our everyday lives. Because the kingdom of heaven is "at hand" or "has come near" through Christ, we have access to pray that all that is true in heaven will be made so on earth.

> What is the most transformational truth about verses 9-10 of the Lord's Prayer for you? Why?

Beginning our prayers by focusing on our own needs, priorities, and concerns is natural. But when we begin instead by lifting high the name and rule of God, we're learning to live in the world the way God intended—as dependent children perfectly at rest in His care.

When You Pray Today

Write your own prayer that begins with a focus on the **name, kingdom, and will of God.** Make a point to begin with Him.

DAY THREE
OUR DAILY SUSTENANCE

Personal prayer is essential to our relationship with Christ, but I want to keep reminding you that the Disciple's Prayer was meant to be prayed in community. When you read the prayer today, pay special attention to the pronouns Jesus used: *our, us, we*. This doesn't mean we shouldn't pray it by ourselves—we should, and I often do, especially when I'm not sure what to pray. But as we continue to study this prayer, keep in mind its communal nature. I hope you will incorporate praying it together with your Bible study group if you're in one.

BEFORE WE GET INTO TODAY'S STUDY, THOUGHTFULLY READ MATTHEW 6:9-13, giving special attention to verse 11. Ask the Holy Spirit to remove anything from your heart and mind that would keep you from being able to hear Him.

Describe the way the focus of the prayer shifts in verse 11.

Why do you think beginning with the "Yours" and then moving to the "ours" is important when we pray? Give this some thought.

In verse 11, Jesus told us to pray for our daily_____.

My dad and brother have been making bread for several years now. Because I am nothing if not a firstborn, I recently joined their bread bandwagon and am now comparing loaves. I currently have two twenty-five-pound bags of grain, one of spelt, and one of hard red wheat berries in my pantry with a wheat mill sitting nearby. At this early stage in my bread career, I would not consider myself even a decent bread maker. I have yet to dabble in sourdough (regularly feeding your culture feels too much like having a puppy), and I don't have any fancy scales or

Before you begin today's study, pray **Psalm 119:18,**

Open my eyes so that I may contemplate wondrous things from your instruction.

pans. But this one thing I can tell you: I have a slice of bread (or three) every morning with my coffee. I adore it.

The fact that I love bread, and you love bread, and we all love bread is not coincidental. It's an enduring, universal staple, which is why Jesus can cover so much real estate of need with just the words *daily bread*. Bread is a symbol of all we deem essential.

For Jesus's Jewish audience in particular, a prayer for daily bread would have also brought to mind a significant time period in Israel's history, a time when God uniquely provided.

> Asking God to give us our "daily bread" not only communicates our dependence on Him to provide our basic needs, but it also reminds us to rely on Him for all of life's provisions.

HOLD YOUR PLACE IN MATTHEW AND READ EXODUS 16:1-5. (This account took place shortly after the Israelites left the bondage of Egypt on their way to the promised land. They struggled in the in-between place of the wilderness, and one of their chief complaints to Moses had to do with their sparse provisions.)

What specifically did God provide for the Israelites in response, and how often did He provide it?

Literal bread, water, and shelter would have also been very real concerns for much of Jesus's first-century audience. And they remain primary concerns for so many in our world today. Whether I'm in the Amazon or Moldova with Justice & Mercy International—two very different cultures and geographical locations—I'm always sobered by how many people struggle to have their basic needs met. Most of us going through this study didn't wake up wondering if we would be able to eat today or if we'd have shelter. But asking God to give us our "daily bread" not only communicates our dependence on Him to provide our basic needs, but it also reminds us to rely on Him for all of life's provisions.

What does praying for daily bread mean to you? What does it represent in your life?

Some of the early church fathers, such as Tertullian, Cyprian, and Augustine, found the practical request for daily bread to be too great a leap from the petitions relating to God's glory that came before it.[14] In other words, they didn't think our mundane needs fit alongside the prayers about God's greatness and kingdom. So they allegorized bread to mean either the Word of God or the Lord's Supper.

Two of the most renowned Reformers, Calvin and Luther, thought just the opposite. They interpreted daily bread literally, including anything that pertained to our basic needs and provisions. In this instance, I agree with the Reformers, and many others, who see the petition for daily bread as Jesus's way of acknowledging how important our physical needs are to our heavenly Father.[15] To me, the vast leap between the glory of God and our physical need for sustenance only further emphasizes His loving condescendence toward us in the person of Jesus.

Something that will help us better understand what "daily bread" stands for is considering the context that surrounds the Lord's Prayer.[16]

READ MATTHEW 6:25-34. Even if this is a familiar passage to you, read it slowly, asking the Holy Spirit to administer these words to your heart.

What were Jesus's first-century listeners worried about (v. 25)?

Jesus alleviated their concerns by pointing to two different aspects of creation. What were they (vv. 26,28)?

What did Jesus tell His listeners to do in relation to the birds of the sky (v. 26)? (Hint: it's the first word of the verse.)

Some of your translations say *look, observe,* or *consider.* The Greek word means *to look intently.*[17] In other words, we're to reflect on how the birds go about their lives, in particular, how they're fed.

What are the three activities birds don't do? Despite the fact that birds aren't capable of these three activities, what does our heavenly Father do for them?

Sowing, reaping, and storing are actions that have to do with our ability to plan. Every spring I sow seeds in my backyard garden. I check the seed packet for the section that tells me the days to maturity so I know when to reap the lettuce, kale, spinach, and tomatoes I've planted. Sadly, my little raised beds don't produce enough for me to store in barns (I'll let you know when I've reached that level), but if I could store them, I would. The point is that we humans have the faculties to plan, save, invest, and freeze the ground beef until we need it for lasagna. The birds can't do this! They live day-to-day, worm-to-appetizing-worm, not because of their planning abilities but because Creator God takes care of their needs.

> If God provides for the birds who can't plan, harvest, or save, how does this encourage you as you pray for God to provide for your daily needs (daily bread)?

Jesus's next example of a wildflower's beauty is meant to be taken alongside the example of the birds.

> The disciples were to "consider" the birds of the sky. What were they to do in relation to the wildflowers?

The CSB translation uses the word *observe* (v. 28). The Greek word means *to learn, examine closely, observe well.*[18] When is the last time you sat for a moment and reflected on some flowers in a field, or from your cut garden, or from—let's be real—the bouquet you bought while getting onions and broccoli from the produce section of the grocery store? Let's consider what Jesus is teaching us.

> Are flowers more or less capable than birds at providing for themselves? What can't flowers do for themselves (v. 28)?

> What is Jesus's argument in verses 29-30? Put it in your own words.

Wildflowers are even less capable of doing for themselves than birds. Whereas birds can fly and gather food and build nests, flowers can't stitch a thread of clothing for themselves. Yet God dresses them even more beautifully than King Solomon. King Solomon was King David's son, the one who built God's holy temple. He was one of Israel's most renowned kings, known for his extraordinary wealth and wisdom. We can only imagine His spectacular clothes. For a modern-day comparison, think of your favorite, most beautifully dressed actress or performer.

Write down the rhetorical questions Jesus asked in verses 26 and 30.

To make His point, Jesus used "lesser to greater" reasoning, a form of argument common in ancient Jewish culture. If God generously feeds the birds and elaborately clothes the wildflowers (lesser), how much more important to Him are you and I (greater)?

Back to our theme of prayer, how do verses 25-34 help clarify what "give us today our daily bread" means (v. 11)?

Daily bread represents God's provision for our needs, which is different from our wants. I believe God delights in our asking for what we want so long as it's not in opposition to His will and ways of righteousness. But I do wonder how often we seek Him for daily wants instead of for daily needs. And how infrequently we thank Him for the countless times He meets our fundamental needs.

What falls under the category of "daily bread" that God has generously provided for you? Make a list and then thank Him for the tangible blessings you wrote down. I am always amazed at how powerful gratitude is in conquering a spirit of discontentment.

If you're like me, you find yourself sifting between wants and needs when you pray, between what you have to have and what you think you have to have. Don't avoid this process. Lean into these questions. Sit for a moment and consider the birds. I can hear them as I write, and maybe you can hear them as you read. Hover over a blooming tulip or a freshly budding rose and observe its beauty and what it didn't exert to get there. Ask the Lord to provide for you all that your daily bread represents and be thankful in prayer for the ways He daily meets your needs. Perhaps you will find that you don't really need some of what you've wanted and that what you never knew you wanted, He wants to give you.

When You Pray Today

End by **praying for daily bread** with a renewed sense of confidence in God's desire to meet your needs.

DAY FOUR
FORGIVE US AS WE FORGIVE

Before you begin today's study, pray **Psalm 119:18,**

Open my eyes so that I may contemplate wondrous things from your instruction.

Forty-eight years after my parents founded Reston Bible Church in a friend's living room in Northern Virginia, we celebrated their last official Sunday. It was a surreal day in many respects. How do you honor nearly half a century of service on a single Sunday morning? Hundreds of friends and family members came out to celebrate, some of whom we've known for decades. The service was full of moving tributes to my parents, and the final video of images of church life that spanned forty-eight years did a number on my mascara. Despite my dignified attempts at holding it together, I could not contain my emotions for all the memories and people.

Looking around that room at all those faces, some of whom I've known since birth, I can tell you one thing: Take forgiveness out of the mix and the whole thing would have been over before it started. Yes, I'm of course talking about the forgiveness Jesus has given His people. But I'm also talking about the forgiveness we extend to one another as a result. The body of Christ can't exist without forgiveness flowing in and out of us. This is why verse 12 of the Lord's Prayer is so essential. Without seeking regular forgiveness from God, our relationship with Him is hindered. And without giving it and receiving it amongst ourselves, we can lose our most precious gift—each other.

> READ MATTHEW 6:9-13, giving special attention to verse 12.

> What do you think is the significance of Jesus placing daily bread and forgiveness next to each other in His prayer?

Perhaps you came up with something similar to John Stott, who wrote "Forgiveness is as indispensable to the life and health of the soul as food is for the body."[19] Just as our physical needs must be met, so our relational ones need tending.

Does forgiveness feel as essential to you as your daily needs being met? Why or why not?

LOOK BACK AT VERSE 12. What two aspects of forgiveness are mentioned?

Notice that Jesus told us to forgive debtors instead of debts. In other words, we're called to forgive people, not their offenses. How does this distinction affect how you pray prayers of forgiveness?

I wonder what comes to mind when you think of the word *debt*. It may have something to do with an outstanding credit card balance or the mortgage on your home. Most of us would like to be debt *free*. Or maybe what comes to mind is a debt someone owes you. In Matthew's Gospel, *debt* is a metaphor for *sin*. When we sin against God, we owe Him a debt because sin is costly.

This is especially problematic for us as sinners because we're incapable of paying God the debt we owe. Here is where the astounding nature of the gospel comes in.

Look up the following references and answer their corresponding questions.

READ 1 PETER 1:18-19. Who paid our ransom and with what currency?

READ ROMANS 6:23. What is the wage or price of sin? And what is the free gift of God?

First John 2:2 says, "He himself is the atoning sacrifice for our sins, and not only for ours, but also for those of the whole world." The word *atonement* here in its simplest form means that Jesus took upon Himself the punishment that was due us.[20] He literally paid the debt we owed God. When we come to Christ and receive the gift of His sacrifice for us, our debt is paid once and for all. God declares us righteous. This is called "justification."

However, our "sanctification" is the process of us becoming more and more like Christ as we daily follow Him. And here's where today's part of the Lord's Prayer comes in. When we sin against God and others, we're to regularly seek His forgiveness, not for our salvation which is already secure in Christ, but for daily cleansing and renewal. This keeps our fellowship with Him free and unhindered.

> Now that we've freshly reflected on the debt we've been forgiven, list any connections you see between receiving forgiveness from God and extending forgiveness to others.

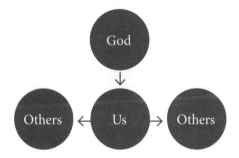

A friend of mine who is quite open about her lack of belief in the Christian faith expressed to me her desire to forgive her parents for the pain they'd caused her as a child. "I want to forgive them; I just can't do it," she explained. She knew the fits of anger that crept up on her were unsustainable. She hated the wedge that unforgiveness put between her and her parents and between her kids and their grandparents. She wanted to be free of the burden but couldn't lay it down.

Because I knew her aversion to Christ, I was racking my brain for a series of forgiveness steps, or a go-to book, but the thing that was remarkably clear to me is that genuine, lasting forgiveness isn't possible without a relationship with the Forgiver. I don't remember being terribly eloquent that day. We were both teary, and I stumbled in my responses, but I remember saying something along the lines of, "I can't give you anything helpful about forgiveness apart from Jesus." We really do need Jesus's help to forgive.

Part of the way we show God we love Him is by forgiving others.

I don't always think of forgiveness in these terms, but
LOOK UP 1 JOHN 4:9-10. How does this passage testify to
this reality?

TURN BACK TO MATTHEW 6 and read verses 14-15.

If you forgive others, your heavenly Father will

_____.

If you don't forgive others, your heavenly Father won't

_____.

What do these verses tell us about the seriousness of forgiving those
who have hurt us?

At first glance, it might seem as though Jesus was teaching that forgiving others is how we earn God's forgiveness. But we know from other portions of Scripture (such as Eph. 2:8-9) that salvation is God's gift to us through Jesus (we just saw this in 1 John 4:9-10). God's forgiveness isn't earned; it's received. At the same time, when we are transformed by Christ's lavish forgiveness of our sins, we will not want to go on harboring bitterness and revenge in our hearts toward those who have hurt us. Now unforgiveness may still feel most natural to us, especially if we have been deeply wounded by someone we loved and trusted. But in light of the forgiveness Jesus has given us, in light of His coming alongside us, we will aim to seek forgiveness even if it goes against our formidable feelings.

Later in Matthew's Gospel, Jesus told a parable about forgiveness that is helpful as we pray for the capacity to forgive others.

READ MATTHEW 18:21-35. How would you sum up Jesus's teaching
on forgiveness here in one sentence? Write it below.

In verse 35, Jesus said we're to forgive others from our _____.

Why is forgiving from our hearts such a challenge?

Forgiveness isn't just something we do or words we say; it's a change that takes place within us. And it can be a process, especially if the wound is deep and the consequences long felt. C. S. Lewis says it well, "The real trouble about the duty of forgiveness is that you do it with all your might on Monday and then find on Wednesday that it hasn't stayed put and all has to be done over again."[21] It's not that the forgiveness we determined in our hearts on "Monday" didn't count; it's that it can be like peeling an onion—there always seems to be another layer. This is why we need to daily come to Jesus. Only Jesus can change our hearts, which is why we can't forgive those who have deeply hurt us without Him.

Let's close by looking at Jesus's own prayer of forgiving others.

> READ LUKE 23:32-34. Notice that Jesus didn't act alone. He involved His Father through prayer when it came to forgiving those who mocked and eventually crucified Him. How does Jesus's prayer impact your own prayers about forgiving others?

Reconciled and flourishing relationships is one of the central themes in Jesus's Sermon on the Mount, and we see it highlighted in the Lord's Prayer. Insofar as it lies with us, we don't want unresolved offenses hindering our fellowship with one another. Forgiving someone, or receiving their forgiveness, doesn't necessarily mean we'll be in relationship with that person. That's OK in many circumstances. But whenever it's possible, we want to be people who seek reconciliation and healing in our relationships (2 Cor. 2:5-11). God's forgiveness for His people and our forgiveness toward one another are what hold our relationships together.

When You Pray Today

Is there an area of sin in your life that you haven't asked the Lord's forgiveness for? If so, pray for it now.

Is there someone in your life you're harboring unforgiveness toward? If so, **pray to forgive.** Place your heartbreak, fears, and concerns in the Lord's hands. He can handle them. And remember, the Spirit of God lives in you, empowering you to forgive as He forgave you. And even when you don't feel like forgiving, He will help you do it.

DAY FIVE

DON'T LET US BE OVERWHELMED BY EVIL

Before you begin today's study, pray **Psalm 119:18,**

Open my eyes so that I may contemplate wondrous things from your instruction.

As we reach the final portion of the Lord's Prayer, I hope you've gained a deeper understanding of each part and that by doing so your own prayers are more firmly grounded. We'll see the themes from Jesus's prayer surface over and over again as we study more prayers from the Bible over the next five sessions.

One of the ways I know I'm praying the Lord's Prayer and not my own is how much it doesn't sound like me in places. I don't mean I disagree with the words or I'm disconnected from the prayer's praises and pleas; it's just that, for example, my first instinct isn't usually to pray for things like protection from evil.

Let me be clear: It's not that I don't think evil exists or that I haven't come up against it at different times in my life. But I think I've been influenced into thinking that "evil" is just a little too dramatic of a word. Must we look for Satan behind every bush? Even for Christ-followers, we may identify with *deliver us from a Target shopping addiction, an extra slice of cheesecake at dinner, and sharing morsels of gossip at work,* but *evil* is just a lot more than what we often think of ourselves as having to contend with.

Yet the older I get, the more astounded I am by the brokenness and plain evil that pervades our life on earth. Wars and violence, racism, families torn apart by abuse and addiction, fraud, stealing, and the overwhelming darkness housed in our personal devices. Not to mention the sin that creeps out of my own heart and the struggles of life in a broken world. This is not to say we should live terrified of evil. Christ who lives within us is greater than the evil one who's working in the world (1 John 4:4). But we need to have our eyes open to the power of evil, to be sober-minded, to actively pray for deliverance from it.

READ MATTHEW 6:9-13, giving special attention to verse 13. Fill out the two parts of this petition:

That God would not bring us into _____.

But _____ us from evil.

So that we can best understand what this means, let's consider some additional passages in Scripture.

READ JAMES 1:13-15. What did James say God will never do?

Where can being drawn away by temptation ultimately lead us?

READ 1 CORINTHIANS 10:13. What two things does Paul teach us about God's activity in our lives when we're tempted?

Given these additional passages, what do you think is the essence of what we're to pray for according to Matthew 6:13?

We must read Matthew 6:13 in light of the fact God doesn't tempt us to sin. This seems contradictory because the first part of the verse is a petition for God to not "bring us into temptation." But the second part, "but *deliver* us from evil" (emphasis mine), helps explain this. If the second half is a prayer to be rescued from evil, then it makes sense that the first half is a request that we not be overwhelmed by temptation which leads to evil. John Stott interprets it this way: "Do not allow us so to be led into temptation that it overwhelms us, but rescue us from the evil one."[22]

Each of us knows our own weakness and tendency to sin. We know what entices us down detrimental paths. Some of my temptations are different from yours and vice-versa. So, when I pray this part of the Lord's Prayer, I'm asking my heavenly Father, my Protector, to keep me from any temptation that would overwhelm me or take me under. Along these lines, I ask Him to deliver me from the sway of the evil one.[23]

PRAY. *Without revisiting past sin in your life and without feeling like you have to be overly detailed, how would you finish this two-part prayer based on what you know about yourself?[24]*

Heavenly Father, lead me not into . . .

Heavenly Father, deliver me from the evil one and his scheme of . . .

READ MATTHEW 7:7-11. Using this passage from later in the Sermon on the Mount for reference, take a moment to write about how different our heavenly Father is from the evil one. Probe beneath the surface.

This is a good time to differentiate between testing and temptation. Whereas the enemy's tempting is for our downfall, God's testing is always for our good.[25] As we just saw in Matthew 7:7-11, He is a good and trustworthy Father.

READ JAMES 1:2-4,12. What does the testing of our faith produce (vv. 3-4)?

What is the benefit of faithfully enduring trials (v. 12)?

How can you tell the difference between a trial and a temptation in your life? Be specific about how you know the difference.

We're to both pray to be delivered from evil as well as contend against it by living according to God's Word.

Trials and hardship, no matter their source, can strengthen our faith and deepen our relationship with Jesus. But temptation is something we should always flee because it can only lead to sin, destruction, and death. These may seem like big, bad Bible words, but it really is true. When temptation turns into sin, it can lead to the most awful places we could have never imagined ending up in. This is why we want to pray that we'll not walk into temptation but that God would rescue us from where it leads—evil. We don't want to play with temptation's fire or see how close we can get to it without actually sinning. We would never take such risks in other areas of our lives.

Let's close with one more passage of Scripture so we can see how Jesus Himself dealt with profound temptation.

READ MATTHEW 4:1-11. What was Jesus's primary defense in combating Satan's temptations?

That Jesus fasted forty days in the wilderness indicates He was also praying since praying and fasting go hand in hand (see Neh. 1:4; Luke 2:37; Acts 14:23).[26] And His use of Scripture to contend with Satan's temptations was another weapon He used. Put simply, Jesus's knowledge of the Word and His praying the Word were two of His greatest protections against the evil one. It seems that Jesus was actively showing us how to walk out His prayer in Matthew 6:13. We're to both pray to be delivered from evil as well as contend against it by living according to God's Word.

Verse 13 of the Lord's Prayer has reawakened me to the seriousness of evil and temptation in my life and our world. I need to get this strong language back into my prayer rotation. I may wish that evil was something I could easily sweep under the carpet, but it is in fact pacing on top of the carpet, like a roaring lion looking for those it can devour (1 Pet. 5:8).

In what areas of your life do you need to be more prayerful regarding temptation and deliverance from the power of the evil one? Write down two or three specific areas where you can start putting this into practice.

We have studied the Lord's Prayer together so that it might become our own. And what a wonderful week it's been. We began by lifting high God's name (Matt. 6:9), and so it feels fitting to end with a similar affirmation included in the New King James Version of the Bible: "For Yours is the kingdom and the power and the glory forever. Amen" (Matt. 6:13). As we continue our study of prayer together, may we learn to bring our praises and requests before the living God. To Him, and only Him, belongs the kingdom of heaven, all the power in the universe, and all the glory, forever and ever. Amen.

When You Pray Today

Close this week's study by putting **Matthew 6:13** into your own words and praying it back to the Lord. If you need help, you can use my words.

Personal Prayer: *Heavenly Father, don't allow life's burdens to be so heavy I give into sin. Don't let temptation be so great it overwhelms me. Instead, rescue me from evil and the evil one. For the power of darkness cannot begin to overcome the light You've placed within me. Help me participate with You in avoiding temptation, never playing with it. And when it springs on me without notice, hold me fast from sin, and ultimately deliver me from Satan's evil agenda in my life and this world.*[27]

WATCH

SESSION TWO

Watch the Session Two video and take notes below.

TO ACCESS THE VIDEO SESSIONS, USE THE INSTRUCTIONS
IN THE BACK OF YOUR BIBLE STUDY BOOK.

Discuss

If you are part of a *When You Pray* Bible study group, use this page to take notes during your group time and to keep a record of prayer requests that are mentioned.

My Heart Rejoices in The Lord

BY JACKIE HILL PERRY

Do you remember the very first prayer you ever prayed? Not necessarily *what* you prayed but *how*?

It's possible your first prayer was adoration. It's even possible your first prayer was imprecatory (prayers for vengeance and justice), although it's unlikely. I'm confident in assuming the first prayer you ever prayed was a petition. Maybe beside your bed as Mama or Daddy knelt nearby, you asked God for something. A better day at school or a good night's sleep. Maybe you didn't grow up Christian, so prayer was as foreign as God had been to you.

Then you got all grown and convicted, so you decided to pray one day. For a new mind, a new heart, and a right spirit. Whatever it was, you needed/wanted something, so you asked God for it. This is by definition what the term *petition* means.

This Week's Prayer

BIBLE PASSAGE
1 Samuel 1:1–2:11

PRAYER TYPE
Prayers of Petition and Thanksgiving

My heart rejoices in the LORD; my horn is lifted up by the LORD. My mouth boasts over my enemies, because I rejoice in your salvation.

1 SAMUEL 2:1

DAY ONE
PETITION

TO BEGIN, READ 1 SAMUEL 1:1–2:11.

Before we spend some time looking at Hannah's prayer of petition in 1 Samuel 1, let's take today to look at other Scriptures that speak to the subject.

Write out each passage:

Matthew 7:7-11

Matthew 21:22

Philippians 4:6

1 John 5:14-15

When you consider these passages, what are your thoughts? Include what encourages you, convicts you, and quite frankly, what scares you about prayers of petition.

Before you begin today's study, pray **PSALM 119:33,**

Teach me, LORD, the meaning of your statutes, and I will always keep them.

PETITION:

"A prayer requesting something of a deity."[1]

Many things can be said about the act of petitioning God in prayer, but one aspect I'd hate for us to miss is that *God wants us to ask Him for things*. Say it with me:

GOD WANTS ME TO ASK HIM FOR THINGS!

It's common for us to respond to the subject of petition from two perspectives.

CYNICISM: "If I ask God for something, He won't answer."

ENTITLEMENT: "If I ask God for something, He must answer."

What is the problem with both views?

The cynic and the entitled believer share the same underlying problem: pride. Cynicism involves the absence of hope and faith. The cynic has concluded that even if she prays, God *will not* respond. Assuming ill motives of God, she's disregarding dozens of Scriptures that declare God *will* and *does* answer prayer. Pride manifests in the entitled Christian in that she has obligated God to answer her prayers instead of obligating herself to be content with God's will. The truth is, God always answers prayer. Sometimes, He answers with a yes. Other times, a no or not yet. All are in fact *answers*.

We all move in-between both extremes on any given day and especially in unique seasons of life. Since that is the case, what we need most is to be reminded of four things that give us an appropriate understanding of petition:

1. The nature of God;

2. The nature of the petitioner;

3. The act of petition;

4. The result of petition.

READ MATTHEW 7:7-11 PRINTED BELOW. After you read over it once, go back through it and:

1. (Circle) repeating words.

2. Underline repeating themes.

3. ✳Put a star next to moral descriptions.

Ask, and it will be given to you. Seek, and you will find. Knock, and the door will be opened to you. For everyone who asks receives, and the one who seeks finds, and to the one who knocks, the door will be opened. Who among you, if his son asks him for bread, will give him a stone? Or if he asks for a fish, will give him a snake? If you then, who are evil, know how to give good gifts to your children, how much more will your Father in heaven give good things to those who ask him.

MATTHEW 7:7-11

What repeated words did you notice?

What repeated themes did you notice?

What moral descriptions did you notice?

Read these for further study on prayer and the will of God:

- Psalm 145:18
- Proverbs 3:5-6
- Micah 6:8
- John 15:7
- John 16:23-24
- Romans 8:27
- Hebrews 13:20-21
- James 4:2-3
- 2 Peter 3:9

One chapter before Matthew 7, Jesus taught His disciples *what* to pray (the Lord's Prayer, which you studied last week). In the text you just read, Jesus taught His disciples *how* to pray. Let's look at how this verse speaks to the nature of God, the nature of the petitioner, the act of petition, and the result of petition.

1. THE NATURE OF GOD

Citing a verse from what you just read in Matthew 7:7-11, explain the nature/character of God.

In this text, God is said to be a "Father" whose location is "heaven." This description is an echo of another verse in Matthew in which God is described the same way. Find it and write the reference here: _____.[2]

Two times in the context of prayer, Jesus referred to God as not merely His Father but the Father of all who are in Christ. What's the significance of recognizing God as Father in relation to petition?

I want you to think about *how you think* when you *pray*. In both Matthew 6:9 and Matthew 7:11, Jesus talked about praying to "your [our] Father in heaven." When you address God, how do you envision Him? I'm not asking if you have a mental image of God in mind when you pray as if believers need a graven image when addressing an invisible God. Rather, consider what name or attribute of God you use and think of most while praying.

When you pray, do you primarily refer to God and thus imagine Him as "Master and Lord"? Or maybe "Savior," "King," or something else? How does the way you address God affect the way you approach Him in prayer?

Considering Jesus's question to His disciples in verses 9-10, if a child asked her parents for bread and got a stone instead, she'd still be hungry. If the child asked her parents for a fish but received a snake, she'd not only be hungry, but perhaps, she'd be harmed. Seeing that "the bread and the stone" and "the snake and the fish" are items that *may* look similar, Jesus was teaching something important about God's nature and thus His motives. **What is it?**

> *God will not mock our prayers, giving us stones for bread or snakes for fish. He will not give us what will harm us, and for that reason He will often answer our prayers differently from what we ask. We do not know what is for our good. He does.*[3]

2. THE NATURE OF THE PETITIONER

Citing a verse from Matthew 7:7-11, explain the nature of the petitioner.

Jesus contrasted the nature of God with the nature of the petitioner to make one principle of prayer plain. What is it?

God is good, all the time. He is holy in His nature. Pure in His wisdom. Loving in His being. Because of original sin, we've inherited a hard heart and a darkened understanding, inclining us toward evil. Yet and still, though we are evil by nature, we have a keen sense of what goodness is and how to give it to those we love. As Jesus laid it out, if we, an evil people, know how to spread goodness, then surely God who is good will always do good to those who ask Him to.

3. THE ACT OF PETITION

Citing a verse from Matthew 7:7-11, explain the act of petition.

In your own words, what are the differences between asking and seeking and knocking?

How do verses 7-8 address (negatively and positively) the perspectives of both the cynic and the entitled believer?

It's OK to be persistent in prayer. To knock on God's door over and over and over again, because truth be told, God doesn't grow tired of our petitions. We grow tired of petitioning. God will answer, in His time, according to His will.

What in your life are you asking God for?

Seeking God to receive?

Knocking to find?

4. THE RESULT OF PETITION

Citing a verse from Matthew 7:7-11, explain the result of petition.

Jesus described the results of petition in six ways. What are they?

1.

2.

3.

4.

5.

6.

How should all of the above inform your faith in petitioning God in prayer?

> What is fundamentally at stake is man's picture of God. God must not be thought of as a reluctant stranger who can be cajoled or bullied into bestowing his gifts (6:7-8), as a malicious tyrant who takes vicious glee in the tricks he plays (7:9-10), or even as an indulgent grandfather who provides everything requested of him. He is the heavenly Father, the God of the kingdom, who graciously and willingly bestows the good gifts of the kingdom in answer to prayer.[4]

 When You Pray Today

Use what you have learned about the **nature of God** and the **purpose of petition** to bring a request before God.

Before you
begin today's
study, pray
PSALM 119:33,

*Teach me,
LORD, the
meaning of
your statutes,
and I will
always keep
them.*

DAY TWO
THE PROBLEM

Unlike "praise" or "adoration," prayers of petition are usually the result of some self-identified problem. When we petition God for provision, the problem is financial lack. If we petition God for wisdom, the problem is we are inclined toward foolishness. If ever we decide to petition God for humility, the problem is that somewhere within us is pride. Every petition is an attempt to overcome a problem.

READ 1 SAMUEL 1.

NOW READ VERSES 1-2 AGAIN. What problem is introduced in verses 1-2?

The narrative opens, and we are introduced to three characters. Elkanah, a man from Ephraim, and his two wives, Hannah and Peninnah. We are not provided with the location of the wives' birth; instead, we are given a descriptor about their relationship to the act of giving birth. Peninnah has children. Hannah does not.

The issue of barrenness isn't unfamiliar at this point in the story line of Scripture. Three matriarchs in Genesis were barren. Who were they?

Why would infertility be considered a problem? Use Scripture and personal experience to flesh out your position.

Infertility is not only troubling on a deeply personal level as described by Hannah (1 Sam. 1:15-16) and Rachel (Gen. 30:1). It's also accompanied by social stigmas. The feelings of shame and guilt related to one's inability to bear children from her own womb are frequently exacerbated within religious communities. Assumptions abound. Perhaps it's a lack of faith on the part of either parent? Slow zeal in finding the right doctors or treatments? For many, someone *must* be blamed for the barrenness, right?

Read how one woman describes the public shame of infertility in our day and age: "On the rare occasions I heard of people who were involuntarily without child, I turned aside, averted my eyes. Such a horror. Now I get averted eyes myself. Friends and family cannot hide that their sorrow is mingled with guilt, guilt that the ordinary blessings of creation were given to them, but not to us."[5]

As it is now, it most likely was in Hannah's day too.

> **Read the passage below and <u>underline</u> the text(s) that would've shaped the way Israel viewed infertility:**

> If you listen to and are careful to keep these ordinances, the Lord your God will keep his covenant loyalty with you, as he swore to your ancestors. He will love you, bless you, and multiply you. He will bless your offspring, and the produce of your land—your grain, new wine, and fresh oil—the young of your herds, and the newborn of your flocks, in the land he swore to your ancestors that he would give you. You will be blessed above all peoples; there will be no infertile male or female among you or your livestock.

> DEUTERONOMY 7:12-14

Women such as Hannah not only had to reckon with their own internal sense of shame but also the societal pressures that assumed their barrenness was a consequence, a curse, or a response from God to their sin. In their world, neither her womb nor God's sovereign choice was the problem; *she* was.

> **LOOK BACK AT 1 SAMUEL 1:3-6. Whom does this passage "blame" for Hannah's infertility? Use Scripture to explain.**

Hannah's body isn't the primary reason she's barren, but even still, that doesn't make her circumstance any easier to bear. If anything, suffering ordained by the hand of God can make matters feel worse. Do you agree or disagree? (No yes or no answers.)

Here now, we are face-to-face with the conflict of sovereignty and suffering, the dynamic that befuddles the strongest and weakest of Saints. It's difficult to comprehend how God, the sovereign King of the universe, the holy and therefore good Lord could *allow* pain. The tension tempts us to explain it away. To take suffering out of the realm of God's dominion by implying that He allows *some* things but not *all* things. Even if that's "comforting," is it true?

Let's look at a few texts. You'll want to use the ESV translation (you can find it at biblegateway.com) to fill in the blanks:

1. For he _____ but he _____; he _____, but his hands _____ (Job 5:18).

2. Who has spoken and it came to pass, unless the Lord has commanded it? Is it not _____

_____

_____ come? (Lam. 3:37-38).

3. See now that I, even I, am he, and there is no God beside me; I _____ and I _____; I _____ and I _____; and there is none that can deliver out of my hand (Deut. 32:39).

4. Is a trumpet blown in a city, and the people are not afraid? Does disaster _____, unless

_____? (Amos 3:6).

Considering the immense suffering that's always happening around us, to us, and within us, those texts might be a bit unsettling. Let's not ignore it or shake it off with superficial contentment though. Let's address our feelings head-on. And yes, it may feel trite or "unspiritual" to take a moment and name emotions, but doing so allows us to deal with our honest thoughts about God as the psalmists and the prophets and even our Lord Jesus did. Ignoring our feelings doesn't make us godlier; it just makes us numb.

> When you think about God being sovereign over suffering, what are the feelings and thoughts that come to mind? Be honest.

The good news is that suffering isn't aimless. God not only allows it, but He also *uses* it.

> READ 2 CORINTHIANS 1:3-9 and explain how suffering was used in Paul's life.

> READ ROMANS 8:18-28 and use it to explain how Christians should reckon with the present reality of suffering.

We have a bird's eye view of Hannah's circumstances. We know what she eventually learned—that the Lord who'd closed her womb was doing it on purpose. He wasn't causing pain aimlessly. He wanted to birth something beautiful in her heart before He allowed it to happen in her womb.

In this passage Israelite faith expresses its supreme paradox and boldest affirmation—the Lord may create social and natural tragedies in order to accomplish his purposes that far outweigh the calamity. The Lord sometimes engineers social tragedies, yet he carries them out "that the work of God might be displayed" (John 9:3). Accordingly, human tragedy can be properly evaluated and appreciated only when viewed with a consideration of the end results and ultimate purposes brought about by God.[6]

R. D. BERGEN

When You Pray Today

Identify a problem you want to take before the Lord. As you **petition God to handle that problem,** ask Him to help you see how He is using (or wants to use) your suffering for His glory.

DAY THREE
THE PATTERN

What happens when God doesn't answer our petitions as quickly as we'd prefer? When the pain continues. When the suffering doesn't let up. When you've prayed for days and then weeks, months, and years go by before there's an answer. In the previous day, we learned that Hannah's barrenness was due to the Lord closing her womb. Barrenness is hard enough as it is, but when a "problem" becomes a "pattern," the problem can become unbearable.

> READ 1 SAMUEL 1:3-8. What clue does the text provide for how long Hannah had been barren? List specific verses.

Put yourself in Hannah's shoes for a moment. How might being barren for that amount of time affect your view of God? What temptations might arise from such a situation?

Read the following passages, (circling) repeated phrases or ideas:

. . . but those who trust in the LORD will renew their strength; they will soar on wings like eagles; they will run and not become weary, they will walk and not faint.

ISAIAH 40:31

Now he told them a parable on the need for them to pray always and not give up.

LUKE 18:1

Before you begin today's study, pray **PSALM 119:33,**

Teach me, LORD, the meaning of your statutes, and I will always keep them.

Let us not get tired of doing good, for we will reap at the proper time if we
don't give up.

GALATIANS 6:9

If you had a hard time finding repeated phrases, it's OK. Bible translations can be tricky.
Two verses contain the same Greek word *enkakein*, which is usually translated as "lose
heart" and is defined as "to faint, be weary."[7]

With that in mind, read back over the three verses and (circle) any
additional repeated phrases.

A serious threat to the heart of the petitioner and her continuing in
faith is the temptation to "lose heart." What might it look like for
Hannah to lose heart?

Consider what you've been petitioning God for. If your requests were
to go unanswered "year by year," what would losing heart look like
for you? Or what does it look like if that's how you feel today?

As we consider the struggle that comes with unanswered prayers, I want us to look at
a familiar gospel narrative—the story of Lazarus. This story is triumphant. A man died
and then Jesus came and raised him from the dead. But don't miss an important piece of
the story. Lazarus died *because* Jesus delayed. Let's read and discover why it is that God
doesn't often act as quickly as we'd prefer.

READ JOHN 11:1-21. There are a lot of references to time in these
verses. The first pivotal mention is in verses 5-6 after Jesus was told that
Lazarus was ill. From these verses, what did Jesus do and for how long?

Verses 14-15 gives us the why. What is it?

Jesus's delay was *on purpose*. He delayed so that He could glorify Himself in a way Lazarus's family might not have wanted but in the way God knew they and the disciples needed. For the sake of their faith and nothing more. Believing for ourselves that God's delay is purposeful will help us to mount up on wings like eagles so that we will run and not be weary and walk and not faint (Isa. 40:31).

> Back to Hannah. Year by year, Hannah went without a child. In what context was she reminded of this? Reread 1 Samuel 1:3-8 to help you answer.

Elkanah is a consistent spiritual leader in his home, albeit the polygamy casts a shadow on the complete purity of his faith. He didn't neglect the yearly trek to Shiloh to worship. Commentators are unclear on exactly what feast Elkanah and his family participated in. What is clear, as described in verses 3-5, is that after they participated in the sacrifices, the entire family sat down to eat. This meal "was the culmination of the pilgrimage. Whereas no offerer ate the meat of his own sin or guilt offering, he was given back a substantial part of his own thanksgiving or 'peace' offering (Lev. 7:11-18), and this meat was enjoyed at the meal in celebration of restored fellowship with God."[8]

> The meat was proportioned according to the amount of children either wife had birthed to ensure that each mother and child had enough.[9] Since that is the case, describe the scenario that Hannah, a childless woman, had to endure, year after year.

> If portions were given according to the amount of children a woman had, what are we to gather from Elkanah giving a "double portion" to Hannah?

Hannah not only had to be reminded of what she didn't have during their meal together; she was provoked by Peninnah because of it. This passage doesn't ignore the emotional toll this had on Hannah.

> Write down every description regarding emotions you see in verses 3-8.

> With everything you know about Hannah's circumstance, the reason for the meal, and the climate of it, what should you make of verse 8?

> READ PSALM 42:3 and explain how David's words might apply to Hannah's behavior.

Hannah didn't refrain from eating because she wasn't hungry. She refrained from eating because she was too sad, too vexed, and too troubled.

Elkanah noticed Hannah's behavior and responded to his wife's emotional state selfishly. As displayed by Job's friends too, we all have a tendency to totally drop the ball in comforting the weary by offering shallow and/or self-centered responses and advice.

> With Scripture in mind, what would've been a better way for Elkanah to comfort his wife? (For example, see John 11:1-15, paying close attention to verses 4 and 15.)

There is a time to speak and a time to be quiet. More often than not, the weary-hearted saint doesn't need words but presence. When the time comes for words to be given, though, tell the truth. The truth is, as the Saints of old used to say, "God may not come when you want Him, but He is always on time." Even if they or even you don't want to believe it, it's true. Knock and it will be opened. Seek and you will find. God will answer according to His will and in His time for He never delays for no reason. It is probable that in your waiting, He is preparing you to see His glory.

> *Yes, the longest delay may yet be "right early," for heaven's clock does not beat at the same rate as our little chronometers. God is "the God of patience," and He has waited for millenniums for the establishment of His kingdom on earth; His "own elect" may learn long-suffering from Him, and need to take to heart the old exhortation, "If the vision tarry, wait for it, for it will surely come, and will not tarry." Yes, God's delays are not delays, but are for our profit that we may always pray and not faint, and may keep alight the flame of the sure hope that the Son of man cometh . . .[10]*

When You Pray Today

What has become a pattern of petition in your life? A prayer you're still waiting on God to answer? As you voice that prayer again today, add David's words in Psalm 42:5 to your prayer—
"I will still praise him, my Savior and my God."

Before you begin today's study, pray **PSALM 119:33,**

Teach me, LORD, the meaning of your statutes, and I will always keep them.

DAY FOUR
THE PETITION

Everybody has problems. Everybody. We live in a messy world surrounded by messy people while living with messy hearts. It's all just a mess. Everyone moves about the world looking for ways to fix the mess. Some folks just work harder to deal with or distract from whatever problems they have. Others default to apathy, self-pity, and sloth-like behavior. Feeling inadequate to do anything, they resort to doing nothing. Hannah had a problem for sure. A problem she wanted to fix. The method she employed may feel counterintuitive, but in fact, she used the strongest weapon one has—prayer.

Hannah refused to eat and thus celebrate restored communion with God. She was sad. On this particular trip, Hannah wept, and then what did she do? She went to the temple to meet with God (1 Sam. 1:9).

> When you have a problem, what do you typically default to? Why?

Barrenness was a "problem" Hannah was technically unable to fix on her own, seeing as the Lord is the One who closed her womb. However, Hannah could have responded in many ways other than prayer. There's a barren woman who preceded Hannah in Old Testament history who attempted to get the child she wanted not by petitioning but by scheming.

> READ GENESIS 16:1-2 and explain why Sarah's decision was problematic.

Sarai took matters into her own hands to "obtain children" (Gen. 16:2). Her action (which she would quickly come to regret) stands in stark contrast to Hannah, who walked right by Eli the priest seated in his place of authority and into the temple of the Lord to meet with God. Surely if God caused her circumstances, He could change them too.

Let's look at Hannah's prayer and focus on three aspects of it—her emotions, her Lord, and her identity.

HANNAH'S EMOTIONS

READ 1 SAMUEL 1:9-18, printed below, and (circle) every word or description regarding Hannah's emotions (for example: *deeply distressed*).

On one occasion, Hannah got up after they ate and drank at Shiloh. The priest Eli was sitting on a chair by the doorpost of the LORD's temple. Deeply hurt, Hannah prayed to the LORD and wept with many tears. Making a vow, she pleaded, "LORD of Armies, if you will take notice of your servant's affliction, remember and not forget me, and give your servant a son, I will give him to the LORD all the days of his life, and his hair will never be cut." While she continued praying in the LORD's presence, Eli watched her mouth. Hannah was praying silently, and though her lips were moving, her voice could not be heard. Eli thought she was drunk and said to her, "How long are you going to be drunk? Get rid of your wine!" "No, my lord," Hannah replied. "I am a woman with a broken heart. I haven't had any wine or beer; I've been pouring out my heart before the LORD. Don't think of me as a wicked woman; I've been praying from the depth of my anguish and resentment." Eli responded, "Go in peace, and may the God of Israel grant the request you've made of him." "May your servant find favor with you," she replied. Then Hannah went on her way; she ate and no longer looked despondent.

Emotions are God-given. They're a part of what it means to be human. We'd be robotic without them. We sometimes feel all over the place because of them, but at the end of the day, we need them. Dan Allender calls emotions "the language of the soul."[11] Just a glance at the psalms, and it's evident that emotions are highlighted as a vital part of prayer.

> "The Psalms propel us into the deepest questions about ourselves, about others, and about God. As we let them expose the depths of our emotion, they will lead us to the God who reveals Himself in the midst of our struggle."[12]

SPEND SOME TIME READING THROUGH PSALM 6, PSALM 38, AND PSALM 42, paying special attention to emotional descriptors.

Are you that honest with God during prayer? If so, what's the motivation? If not, what's the hesitation?

Our problems are too big and our feelings are too strong for us to enter God's presence with pretense. The psalmists and Hannah model for us how to bring our entire selves to the feet of God.

HANNAH'S LORD

How we begin our prayers says a lot about us. We can either begin with a problem or with a Person. We've established how when Jesus taught the disciples to pray, He told them to begin, "Our Father in heaven, your name be honored as holy" (Matt. 6:9). When Jesus spoke with God on the cross, His first words were "My God, My God" (Mark 15:34). Hannah's petition opens with "LORD of Armies" (1 Sam. 1:11) Beginning with God's personal name immediately affects our posture in prayer, humbling us, and our power in prayer, encouraging us.

Where in 1 Samuel 1 have we seen LORD of Armies (or LORD of hosts) mentioned before?

Verse 3 is the first use of the name *LORD of Armies* in Scripture. The meaning of it "expresses the infinite resources and power which are at the disposal of God as he works on behalf of his people."[13]

With Hannah's situation in mind, what may be the reason Hannah addressed God as "LORD of Armies" when praying?

The name of God we employ in prayer inspires reverence, and it functions as a reminder. If God is indeed the LORD of Armies, then He is sovereign. He is powerful. He is in control. And if that is the case, then there is no circumstance I can bring to His feet that He doesn't have the ability to change.

How might your prayers change if you were intentional in how you addressed God? List a few specific examples that come to mind.

HANNAH'S IDENTITY

READ 1 SAMUEL 1:11. What word did Hannah use to describe herself three different times in this verse?

The term Hannah used that is translated as *servant* typically describes a female "slave" or "handmaid." It refers to a subjugated position, one of submission to a higher authority.[14]

Consider how Hannah addressed God and how she referred to herself. What was happening in Hannah's heart, and how was that influencing the way she prayed?

READ VERSE 11 AGAIN, ALONG WITH JAMES 4:2-3. How does Hannah's vow reflect the opposite of James's rebuke?

To think that Hannah, a barren and grieving woman, would ask God for a son and then in the same breath vow to give this son back to God is shocking. Usually, when we want something badly, we make no promises to return it to sender. (Which is a part of the problem.) If the gift was *received*, then the gift has a *source*.

Everything we have is a gift from God, the LORD of Armies.

Whether it be children, money, marriage, friendships, health, the ability to speak and walk and dance and laugh or preach, sing, or whatever, *EVERYTHING* is a gift from the Father of lights. Here, Hannah recognized something we are quick to forget: Whenever God answers our prayers, giving us what we've asked for, figuratively and literally speaking, we must give it all right back to God, for our good and His glory. Nothing we have is ultimately ours anyway.

> Whatever it is that you've been petitioning God for, are you willing to surrender it right back to God? Why or why not? Be honest with yourself as you think about this question.

When You Pray Today

Set aside some time right now or later today to sit with God.

1. Be **emotionally honest** with God.

2. Look through the Scriptures and find an **attribute or name of God** that applies to your circumstances.

3. Ask God to **change your heart,** giving you the humility needed to be content with how God answers your prayer, as well as the humility needed to give Him back everything you've received.

DAY FIVE
THE PRAISE

It's a common courtesy to tell a person "thank you" for doing something nice or considerate. If someone opens the door for us or buys us a gift, we would dare say nothing unless we're fine with being rude. Most people understand how thanking someone for something is a way to acknowledge and/or honor him or her. We do it for the most menial of gestures, so how much more should we give thanks to God?

Hannah asked God for a son. God remembered her by opening her womb and blessing her with one, and her posture from beginning to end was one of thankfulness and praise. Before you look at her example though, I want you to consider something else first.

Write down the following passages:

Psalm 106:1

Philippians 4:4-6

Colossians 4:2

1 Thessalonians 5:18

Teach me, LORD, the meaning of your statutes, and I will always keep them.

What do you learn about thankfulness from these verses?

READ ROMANS 1:18-21. What does this text have to say about being unthankful, including the kind of people that represent it? What happens as a result?

READ DANIEL 4:28-37. Explain the pride of Nebuchadnezzar and how it shows up in your own life.

The enemy of thankfulness is self-exalting arrogance (v. 30). If and when we believe that what we have or what we've done is by virtue of our abilities alone, thankfulness will be replaced by boastfulness.

What do you have that you didn't receive? If, in fact, you did receive it,

why do you boast as if you hadn't received it?

1 CORINTHIANS 4:7

NOW READ 1 SAMUEL 1:20-28. What verses offer insight into Hannah's response to God before and after He gave her a son?

Even Samuel's name memorialized Hannah's petition. Using a specific verse, explain how I came to that conclusion.

Being a woman of her word, Hannah fulfilled her vow to the Lord to give Samuel "to the LORD all the days of his life" (v. 11). Waiting until he was weaned (about three years old), she then took him to Shiloh "to appear in the LORD's presence and to stay there permanently" (v. 22).

Although it's not explicitly mentioned in the text, Hannah's vow and the fulfillment of it didn't happen without her husband Elkanah's consent. Displaying deep affection for his wife and God, Elkanah didn't veto her vow, though he had every right to. "Although the Torah explicitly gave him the right to nullify Hannah's vow regarding Samuel's service in the Shiloh sanctuary (cf. Num 30:10–15), he chose instead to confirm her vow to the Lord, even though it meant losing the firstborn son from his beloved wife's womb."[15]

> Looking at verses 25-28 and paying special attention to repetition, who and what was in the forefront of Hannah's mind as it relates to Samuel?

> When God answers your prayers, what is your typical response?

> READ 1 SAMUEL 2:1-11. Choosing not to rejoice solely in the birth of her son, in whom did Hannah ultimately take joy?

> How can we cultivate a heart that loves the Giver more than the gift? List some specific ways you can do this in prayer.

Hannah's prayer in 1 Samuel 2 begins with praise, and as it continues, it explores several themes, primarily how God deals with the disadvantaged and vulnerable in contrast to how He deals with the proud and arrogant.

The **LORD** *is* **EXALTED**	¹My heart rejoices in the LORD; my horn is lifted up by the LORD. My mouth boasts over my enemies, because I rejoice in your salvation. ²There is no one holy like the LORD. There is no one besides you! And there is no rock like our God.
The **BOASTING** *of the* **ARROGANT**	³Do not boast so proudly, or let arrogant words come out of your mouth, for the LORD is a God of knowledge, and actions are weighed by him.
The **HUMBLING** *of the* **PROUD** *&* **EXALTATION** *of the* **WEAK**	⁴The bows of the warriors are broken, but the feeble are clothed with strength. ⁵Those who are full hire themselves out for food, but those who are starving hunger no more. The woman who is childless gives birth to seven, but the woman with many sons pines away. ⁶The LORD brings death and gives life; he sends some down to Sheol, and he raises others up. ⁷The LORD brings poverty and gives wealth; he humbles and he exalts. ⁸He raises the poor from the dust and lifts the needy from the trash heap. He seats them with noblemen and gives them a throne of honor.
The **JUDGMENT** *of the* **LORD** *&* **EXALTATION** *of the* **KING**	For the foundations of the earth are the LORD's; he has set the world on them. ⁹He guards the steps of his faithful ones, but the wicked perish in darkness, for a person does not prevail by his own strength. ¹⁰Those who oppose the LORD will be shattered; he will thunder in the heavens against them. The LORD will judge the ends of the earth. He will give power to his king; he will lift up the horn of his anointed.

1 SAMUEL 2:1-10

Up until this point, there haven't been any kings in Israel. Whom might Hannah be referring to in verse 10?

Much scholarly discussion has centered around Hannah's use of the terms king and anointed (Hb. melek and mĕšîaḥ) in her prayer. Many scholars judge these words to be anachronistic, since Israel obviously had no king at the time. However, it is possible that the words are (1) allusions to the office of kingship mentioned in the Torah (cf. Deut 17:15), (2) references to local Israelite rulers (cf. Judg 9:6), (3) prophetic of the Davidic dynasty (cf. Gen 49:10–12), or (4) references to an anticipated, eschatological figure. The close parallels between Hannah's Prayer and Mary's Song (Luke 1:46–55) suggest that the first-century Christian community considered the entire passage, and especially the phrases "his king" and "his anointed," to be prophetic references to Jesus Christ and his ministry.[16]

Jesus told us that the Scriptures, including the Old Testament, testify about Him (John 5:39). It shouldn't surprise us then that Hannah's prayer, the prayer of a once barren woman, contains a messianic reference to Jesus. Who was a boy, born not to a barren woman but a virgin (Matt. 1:23). Who would "live before the Lord" all the days of His life, functioning as Prophet, Priest, and King. Dying for sinners, including the weak and the vulnerable, reconciling them to God, so they too could "live before Him." All of which was a gift. The Savior and the salvation. What Hannah did, the Father did too. He gave up His Son so that all who are spiritually barren may bear much fruit (John 15:5-8). And for this, we are eternally thankful.

He did not even spare his own Son but gave him up for us all. How will he not also with him grant us everything?
ROMANS 8:32

When You Pray Today

Write a prayer of thankfulness to God. He is worthy!

WATCH

SESSION THREE

Watch the Session Three video and take notes below.

TO ACCESS THE VIDEO SESSIONS, USE THE INSTRUCTIONS
IN THE BACK OF YOUR BIBLE STUDY BOOK.

78

Discuss

If you are part of a *When You Pray* Bible study group, use this page to take notes during your group time and to keep a record of prayer requests that are mentioned.

Your Works Are Wondrous

BY JEN WILKIN

P salm 139 is one of David's best-known psalms, thanks in large part to verse 14: "I praise you, for I am fearfully and wonderfully made (ESV)." Perhaps no other psalm has been as frequently referenced to demonstrate our value as image bearers. But if we aren't careful, in our familiarity with one beautiful verse, we can hurry by the greater beauty of the psalm as a whole. David does celebrate that we are skillfully and miraculously made, but his overall focus is on God—adoration of God for who He is and petition that God would act.

This psalm is an example of a prayer of adoration, a term we tend to link to the idea of love. But in relation to prayer, to *adore* is "to worship, revere, and honor." When we think about petitioning God, we may think in terms of making prayer requests for God to act in specific ways. But in Psalm 139, we will see modeled a form of petition we sometimes avoid. Adoration and petition are linked in the prayer in a way we can learn from. The psalmist first declares who God is and responds to that declaration with a specific request of what God must do.

When our prayers begin with adoring God, we make different requests than we otherwise might. John Calvin famously reflected that the knowledge of God and the knowledge of self always go hand in hand.[1] Meditating on and proclaiming God's excellencies causes us to see our weaknesses and failings in a different light. A better light. As you spend time in this psalm, notice how its example shapes your own prayer, both in your adoration and your asking.

One more note before you begin. If you're unfamiliar with my study method, this week's personal study will likely feel a bit different than others. I want you to "dwell in the 'I don't know'" as you study, so I've saved most of my thoughts and commentary for the teaching video. The questions are intended to help you think through interpretive issues on your own, but don't worry—the video will address any lingering uncertainty you might have.

This Week's Prayer

BIBLE PASSAGE
Psalm 139

PRAYER TYPE
Prayers of Adoration

WHEN OUR PRAYERS BEGIN WITH ADORING GOD, WE MAKE DIFFERENT REQUESTS THAN WE OTHERWISE MIGHT.

I will praise you because I have been remarkably and wondrously made. Your works are wondrous, and I know this very well.

PSALM 139:14

DAY ONE
GOD KNOWS

READ THROUGH PSALM 139 FROM START TO FINISH.
A copy of it is provided on pages 104–105 for you to
mark.

Draw a [bracket] to mark the portion of the
psalm that focuses on adoration (worship, reverence,
honor).

How many verses are devoted to adoration?

Draw a [bracket] to mark the portion of the psalm that
focuses on petition (asking God to act).

How many verses are devoted to petition?

Using a red pen, circle every occurrence of *you* or *your*
that references God. Then read the psalm aloud from
start to finish, emphasizing each word you circled.

What portions of the psalm minister to you most on this
initial reading? Why?

What portions cause discomfort? Why?

Before you
begin today's
study, pray
PSALM 119:34,

*Help me
understand
your
instruction,
and I will
obey it
and follow it
with all my
heart.*

In your typical prayers, what proportion do you spend adoring God? What proportion do you spend petitioning Him? What might your answer indicate you believe to be the central purpose of prayer?

NOW LOOK AT PSALM 139:1-4. Notice the repeated idea in these verses. With a green <u>underline</u>, mark every verb related to *knowing* in these first four verses.

Draw a line to match each verse to what God knows:

Verse 2a	my thoughts
Verse 2b	my daily habits
Verse 3	my words
Verse 4	my location

What word is repeated in both verse 3 and verse 4 to indicate the extent of what God knows? _____
Mark it with a blue wavy <u>underline</u>.

God holds perfect knowledge of past, present, and future.

From David's poetic words, what are we to understand about how much God knows? Fill in the blank:

God knows _____.

Theologians refer to God's complete and total knowledge as His *omniscience*. He holds perfect knowledge of past, present, and future. (For a list of the attributes of God in Psalm 139, see page 103.)

As A. W. Tozer notes,

God knows instantly and effortlessly all matter and all matters, all mind and every mind, all spirit and all spirits, all being and every being, all creaturehood and all creatures, every plurality and all pluralities, all law and every law, all relations, all causes, all thoughts, all mysteries, all enigmas, all feeling, all desires, every unuttered secret, all thrones and dominions, all personalities, all things visible and invisible in heaven and in earth, motion, space, time, life, death, good, evil, heaven, and hell.[2]

LOOK UP THE FOLLOWING VERSES and note how each affirms God's omniscience:

Job 37:16	
Psalm 44:20-21	
Psalm 147:5	
Isaiah 40:27-28	

Everything you and I know we have learned. Think of the person whom you have learned from the most in your life. Who is it?

What made that person a source of learning for you?
Check all that apply:

☐ She/he knew more than I did.

☐ She/he had greater understanding and experience than I did.

☐ She/he had more wisdom than I did.

Now think about God. Can anyone (or anything) teach God? Why or why not? Look up Romans 11:33-35 to help with your answer.

How is the truth that God knows all things—including our habits, thoughts, location, and words—a deep source of *comfort* for us?

How does it change the way we view ourselves and how much we know?

How should it change the way we pray?

When You Pray Today

Today you saw that God is:

OMNISCIENT: He knows everything, past, present, and future—all potential and real outcomes, all things micro and macro.

Fill in the following statement:
*Knowing that God is **omniscient** shows me that I am*

_____.

Use that statement as a starting point for a wrap-up prayer of adoration.

DAY TWO
GOD SEES

NOW LOOK AT PSALM 139:5-6.

At first glance, we might think verse 5 is referring to God's surrounding presence. But let's look a little closer. Compare verse 5 in the ESV and the NLT. Fill in the missing words:

(ESV) You hem me in, _____ and _____, and lay your hand _____.

(NLT) You go _____ me and _____ me. You place your hand of blessing _____.

NOW LOOK UP REVELATION 1:8 and fill in the blanks for God's description of Himself:

(CSB) "I am the Alpha and the Omega," says the Lord God, "the one who ____, who _____, and who _____, the Almighty."

NOW LOOK UP ROMANS 11:36 and note Paul's words about God:

(CSB) For _____ him and _____ him and _____ him are all things. To him be the glory _____. Amen.

Based on the similar word patterns of Romans 11:36 and Revelation 1:8, what is David confessing to be true about God in Psalm 139:5?

Before you begin today's study, pray **PSALM 119:34,**

Help me understand your instruction, and I will obey it and follow it with all my heart.

Fill in the missing word in Jeremiah 10:10a to help with your answer:

(CSB) But the LORD is the true God; he is the living God

and _____ King.

Using a dictionary, look up the word you wrote for your previous answer and write a definition for it:

Consider Tozer's words on God's eternality:

Because God lives in an everlasting now, He has no past and no future. When time-words occur in the Scriptures they refer to our time, not to His. When the four living creatures before the throne cry day and night, "Holy, holy, holy, Lord God Almighty, which was, and is, and is to come," they are identifying God with the flow of creature-life with its familiar three tenses; and this is right and good, for God has sovereignly willed so to identify Himself. But since God is uncreated, He is not himself affected by that succession of consecutive changes we call time.

God dwells in eternity but time dwells in God. He has already lived all our tomorrows as He has lived all our yesterdays.[3]

"[God] has already lived all our tomorrows as He has lived all our yesterdays."

A. W. TOZER

LOOK UP THE FOLLOWING VERSES and note how each celebrates God's eternality:

Psalm 90:2	
Psalm 102:12	
Isaiah 41:4	

Reflecting on God's infinite knowledge and eternal nature, what recognition does David have about his own comprehension skills in Psalm 139:6?

How is the truth that God is eternal a deep source of *comfort* for us?

How does it change the way we view ourselves, as those created on purpose to be in submission to time?

How should it impact the way we pray?

NOW READ VERSES 7-12. With a green <u>underline</u>, mark every place God is said to be.

Draw a line to match each verse with a description of where God is:

Verse 8a   light

Verse 8b   east

Verse 9a   high

Verse 9b   darkness

Verse 11a   low

Verse 11b   west

What is the obvious answer to the questions posed in verse 7?

LOOK UP THE FOLLOWING VERSES and note what you learn about where God is:

1 Kings 8:27	
Jeremiah 23:23-24	
Isaiah 66:1	
Acts 17:27-28	

What assurance is offered in Psalm 139:10?

LOOK UP THE FOLLOWING VERSES and note what you learn about the hand that holds you wherever you go:

Exodus 15:6	
Psalm 89:13	
Psalm 98:1	
Isaiah 48:13	

We call the reality of God's unlimited location His *omnipresence*. A. W. Tozer says, "God is indeed there. He is there as He is here and everywhere, not confined to tree or stone, but free in the universe, near to everything, next to everyone, and through Jesus Christ immediately accessible to every loving heart."[4]

Look up the word *omnipresent* in a dictionary and write a definition for it.

How many places can God be at the same time?

How many places can you be at the same time?

How is the truth that God is omnipresent a deep source of *comfort* for us?

How should it impact the way we pray?

 When You Pray Today

Today you saw that God is:

ETERNAL: God is not limited by time; He exists outside of time.

OMNIPRESENT: God is fully present everywhere.

Knowing that God is **eternal** *shows me that I am*
_____.

Knowing that God is **omnipresent** *shows me that I am*
_____.

Use that statement as a starting point for a wrap-up prayer of adoration.

Before you begin today's study, pray **PSALM 119:34,**

Help me understand your instruction, and I will obey it and follow it with all my heart.

DAY THREE
GOD DOES

NOW LOOK AT PSALM 139:13-16. With a green underline, mark every word describing God's creative work.

David praises God as the uncreated Creator, the One who gives life but who receives it from no one. God is self-existent. God is our origin, and He is the origin of all things. Again, Tozer helps us here:

> Origin is a word that can apply only to things created. When we think of anything that has origin we are not thinking of God. God is selfexistent, while all created things necessarily originated somewhere at some time. Aside from God, nothing is self-caused.[5]

LOOK UP THE FOLLOWING VERSES and note what you learn about the creative work of God:

Genesis 1:1	
John 1:1-4	
2 Corinthians 5:17	
Colossians 1:15-17	
Revelation 4:11	

How does the fact that God made everything and is present everywhere help explain how God knows everything?

If God made everything, to whom does everything belong? LOOK UP PSALM 24:1 to help with your answer.

What impact does this have on the way Christians think about caring for what God has made?

Imagine you buy a painting at an estate sale for twenty dollars and later discover it is a Rembrandt. What would happen to your understanding of the value of the painting based on who created it?

How does our value of others change when we consider who created them?

How is the truth that God is Creator a deep source of *comfort* for us?

How should it impact the way we pray?

NOW LOOK AT PSALM 139:17-18. As he did in verse 6, what does David marvel at as he meditates on God's character?

☐ God is easily understood.
☐ God's thoughts are limitless.

LOOK UP THE FOLLOWING VERSES and note what each has to say about limits and God:

Job 11:7-9	
Psalm 119:96	
Psalm 147:5	
Isaiah 40:28	

Because God is limitless, He is unable to be fully comprehended by a limited human mind. The Bible reveals to us all that is necessary for life and godliness with regard to the knowledge of God, but the number of things that are true about Him is infinite. C. H. Spurgeon shows us how the recognition of an incomprehensible God should impact us:

> *There is something exceedingly improving to the mind in a contemplation of the Divinity. It is a subject so vast, that all our thoughts are lost in its immensity; so deep, that our pride is drowned in its infinity. Other subjects we can compass and grapple with; in them we feel a kind of self-contentment, and go on our way with the thought, "Behold I am wise." But when we come to this master science, finding that our plumbline cannot sound its depth, and that our eagle eye cannot see its height, we turn away with the thought, "I am but of yesterday and know nothing."[6]*

The number of things that are true about God is infinite.

LOOK UP THE FOLLOWING VERSES and note what each has to say about our ability to understand God:

Psalm 145:3	
Psalm 147:5	
Romans 11:33-35	

Though God is not limited in any way, shape, or form, humans are limited by design. Though God cannot be fully comprehended by finite humans, humans can be (and are) fully comprehensible to God. How is it good news that God is unlimited? How is it good news that God is bigger than human understanding?

Today you saw that God is:

INCOMPREHENSIBLE: God is beyond our understanding. We can comprehend Him in part but not in whole.

INFINITE: God has no limits in His person or on His power.

SELF-EXISTENT: God depends on nothing and no one to give Him life or existence.

Knowing that God is **infinite** *shows me that I am*
_____.

Knowing that God is **incomprehensible** *shows me that I am*
_____.

Knowing that God is **self-existent** *shows me that I am*
_____.

Use those statements as a starting point for a wrap-up prayer of adoration.

DAY FOUR
GOD IS HOLY

NOW LOOK AT PSALM 139:19-22.

David now turns from adoration to petition. But what he asks for is, at first glance, unexpected and disorienting to our modern ears. How are we to learn from David's cries of hatred and calls for bloodshed?

Compare verses 19-20 in the CSB and ESV.

CSB	ESV
¹⁹ God, if only you would kill the wicked—	¹⁹ Oh that you would slay the wicked, O God!
you bloodthirsty men, stay away from me—	O men of blood, depart from me!
²⁰ who invoke you deceitfully.	²⁰ They speak against you with malicious intent;
Your enemies swear by you falsely.	your enemies take your name in vain.

How are the enemies of God described?

Which of the Ten Commandments do they break?

Before you begin today's study, pray
PSALM 119:34,

Help me understand your instruction, and I will obey it and follow it with all my heart.

Compare verses 21-22 in the CSB and ESV.

CSB	ESV
²¹ LORD, don't I hate those who hate you, and detest those who rebel against you? ²² I hate them with extreme hatred; I consider them my enemies.	²¹ Do I not hate those who hate you, O LORD? And do I not loathe those who rise up against you? ²² I hate them with complete hatred; I count them my enemies.

How does David feel about the enemies of God?

What does he pledge in verse 22b?

"I consider them _____ enemies."

When David wrote Psalm 139, he was facing flesh and blood enemies who wanted to destroy him. But what about us? Look up Ephesians 6:11-12 and fill in the blanks:

For our _____ is _____ against _____ and _____ (v. 12a).

In light of this spiritual truth, what should we hate with complete hatred? What should we ask God to put to death? LOOK UP THE FOLLOWING VERSES and note what you find:

Romans 8:13	
Galatians 5:24	
Colossians 3:5-6	

What is another way to think about putting sin to death? Look up
1 John 3:2-3 to help with your answer:

And everyone who has this hope in him _____ himself just as he

[Christ] is _____ (v. 3).

After an extended confession of the transcendent glory of God, David
responds with hatred of what God hates. What might we learn from this?
How does meditating on God's character reorient us to hate what He
hates (specifically, our sin)?

When You Pray Today

Today you saw that God is:

HOLY: God is perfect, pure, and without sin.

*Knowing that God is **holy** shows me that I am*

_____.

Use that statement as a starting point for a wrap-up prayer of adoration.

Help me understand your instruction, and I will obey it and follow it with all my heart.

DAY FIVE
GOD IS TO BE ADORED

NOW LOOK AT PSALM 139:23-24.

There are no explicit "you's" to mark in these final verses, but they are implied in each of David's six closing pleas. Write them in red in parentheses at the beginning of each statement.

Example: *(You) Search me, God, and (You) know my heart . . .*

Mark the answer that best describes the six pleas in verses 23-24:

☐ They each request something different.

☐ They all request the same thing.

What explanation would you give for why David writes in this manner?

COMPARE VERSE 23 WITH VERSE 1. What connection do you find?

What is David's assessment of being searched and known by God?

☐ He finds it something to avoid.

☐ He finds it something to desire on an ongoing basis.

When you think about God searching you and knowing you—seeing with complete clarity every thought, word, and deed—how do you feel?

What wrong thinking makes us want to avoid the searching gaze of God?

LOOK UP ROMANS 8:38-39 and note the great comfort it offers the believer.

David closes with another thought that connects back to the beginning of the psalm. Compare Psalm 139:24 with verse 3. In both verses, mark the word *way* with a blue <u>underline</u>. How do the two ideas pair with one another?

How does meditating on God's holiness, omniscience, eternality, omnipresence, self-existence, limitlessness, and incomprehensibility help us to walk "in the everlasting way" (v. 24)? How does it help us to turn from the wide path of folly and walk the narrow path of holiness?

When You Pray Today

Review the attributes of God of Psalm 139 on the next page. Then, write your own **prayer of adoration and petition** informed by David's prayer.

ATTRIBUTES OF GOD IN PSALM 139

ETERNAL: God is not limited by time; He exists outside of time.

HOLY: God is perfect, pure, and without sin.

INFINITE: God has no limits in His person or on His power.

INCOMPREHENSIBLE: God is beyond our understanding. We can comprehend Him in part but not in whole.

OMNIPRESENT: God is fully present everywhere.

OMNISCIENT: God knows everything, past, present, and future—all potential and real outcomes, all things micro and macro.

SELF-EXISTENT: God depends on nothing and no one to give Him life or existence.

PSALM 139 (CSB)

¹LORD, you have searched me and known me.

²You know when I sit down and when I stand up;

you understand my thoughts from far away.

³You observe my travels and my rest;

you are aware of all my ways.

⁴Before a word is on my tongue,

you know all about it, LORD.

⁵You have encircled me;

you have placed your hand on me.

⁶This wondrous knowledge is beyond me.

It is lofty; I am unable to reach it.

⁷Where can I go to escape your Spirit?

Where can I flee from your presence?

⁸If I go up to heaven, you are there;

if I make my bed in Sheol, you are there.

⁹If I fly on the wings of the dawn

and settle down on the western horizon,

¹⁰even there your hand will lead me;

your right hand will hold on to me.

¹¹If I say, "Surely the darkness will hide me,

and the light around me will be night"—

¹²even the darkness is not dark to you.

The night shines like the day;

darkness and light are alike to you.

¹³For it was you who created my inward parts;

you knit me together in my mother's womb.

¹⁴I will praise you

because I have been remarkably and wondrously made.

Your works are wondrous,

and I know this very well.

¹⁵My bones were not hidden from you

when I was made in secret,

when I was formed in the depths of the earth.

¹⁶Your eyes saw me when I was formless;

all my days were written in your book and planned

before a single one of them began.

¹⁷God, how precious your thoughts are to me;

how vast their sum is!

¹⁸If I counted them,

they would outnumber the grains of sand;

when I wake up, I am still with you.

¹⁹God, if only you would kill the wicked—

you bloodthirsty men, stay away from me—

²⁰who invoke you deceitfully.

Your enemies swear by you falsely.

²¹LORD, don't I hate those who hate you,

and detest those who rebel against you?

²²I hate them with extreme hatred;

I consider them my enemies.

²³Search me, God, and know my heart;

test me and know my concerns.

²⁴See if there is any offensive way in me;

lead me in the everlasting way.

WATCH
SESSION FOUR

Watch the Session Four video and take notes below.

TO ACCESS THE VIDEO SESSIONS, USE THE INSTRUCTIONS
IN THE BACK OF YOUR BIBLE STUDY BOOK.

106

Discuss

If you are part of a *When You Pray* Bible study group, use this page to take notes during your group time and to keep a record of prayer requests that are mentioned.

How Long, O Lord?

BY JENNIFER ROTHSCHILD

Hey there, sister! My name is Jennifer, and I'm eager to explore another form of prayer with you this week. So far, Kelly taught us about praying like Jesus. The Lord's Prayer honors God's name as holy and gives us a model for when we pray. Then, Jackie led us through prayers of petition and praise, and we just got done studying with Jen about praying the attributes of God and how they shape what we ask of God. Wow.

Now it's time to lament! I know that doesn't sound very upbeat, but it sounds a lot like our heartbeat, doesn't it? Life often hurts, and we need to know how to pray when it does.

So, let's dive into these dark waters where we'll discover incredible light just below the surface.

This Week's Prayer

BIBLE PASSAGE
Psalm 3; 13; 79, and more

PRAYER TYPE
Prayers of Lament

Lord, teach us Your Word on how to lament and draw our hearts to trust You with our pain. In Jesus's name, amen.

But I have trusted
in your faithful love;
my heart will rejoice
in your deliverance.
I will sing to the LORD
because he has treated
me generously.

PSALM 13:5-6

DAY ONE

IT'S OK TO LAMENT

TO BEGIN, READ ALL OF PSALM 13.

Today I want to introduce you to the theme of lament by going to an imaginary therapy session. You're the therapist, and your client, David (yes, that David—the psalmist, the shepherd, the king), just showed up to unload his troubles through the words of Psalm 13:1-4, the prayer of lament we will focus on today. You must be a very good therapist to have the king of Israel as a client!

Imagine in your first session you learn some parts of your client's backstory.

READ 2 SAMUEL 13 AND 15 (or at least skim the chapters) for part of David's story.

Not pretty, right? Talk about family problems. Rape. Murder. Estrangement. Rebellion. Betrayal. David had to flee for his life. All that is painfully true, and it's just a snippet of his story. We don't know for certain that Psalm 13 was penned following the events of 2 Samuel 13 and 15 (it could have been following another season of awfulness), but fifth-century theologian Theodoret believed it was.[1]

With some knowledge of your client's history, you pull out your notebook to take some notes on what David says. You're not just listening to his words, though; you're also assessing how he's feeling. Listen for the emotion tucked under and woven through his words.

READ PSALM 13:1-4 as if David is sharing it with you in a session or as if he is praying it right there with you in your office so you can feel the weight of every word.

Now put on your analyst hat and describe what he was feeling and thinking. What was David's complaint against God in verse 1?

Before you begin today's study, pray **PSALM 119:145,**

I call with all my heart; answer me, LORD. I will obey your statutes.

What emotions and conditions did David call out in verse 2?

What needs did David express in verse 3?

What does it seem David believed in verse 4? And what was he asking of God in that verse?

After your session with David comes to an end, you sit quietly and review your notes. At that moment, you realize you've felt like David before. Or maybe you feel like him right now.

Describe a time when you felt like David in Psalm 13:1-4.

I wonder if what you just wrote brought up feelings of hopelessness or helplessness. Did it feel bleak? Did you feel overlooked? Fearful? Sad? Grieved?

What emotions went along with that situation? What emotions do you still feel looking back on it?

We've all felt loss, grief, fear, and despair. And we've all cried out, "How long, Lord?" from the depth of our pain.

When we're in the hard middle of suffering, it doesn't feel like it has a short shelf life. When we're gutted by sorrow, blindsided by loss, or worn down by injustice, we can feel like suffering will outlast our fortitude. And we can even wonder if maybe, just maybe, suffering will even outlast God's commitment to us.

So, what do we do when we feel like that?

We lament.

> **Jot down a dictionary definition of lament.**
>
> **To lament is:**

When we lament, we express grief, sorrow, or regret. Prayers of lament can show up as one voice lifting a flood of words, two or three praying on their knees together, or even a dirge sung by a choir.

Psalm 13 is a psalm of lament, and it gives us a beautiful and brutal example of what grief, loss, or despair sounds like in prayer.

Before we deal with more of the feelings that prompt lament, let's nail down a few facts.

FACTS ABOUT LAMENT

- As a genre, lament shows up in all sorts of ways in the Bible: prophetic, liturgical, and narrative. (See Isa. 63:7–64:12; Jer. 14:17-22; 20:7-11; Lam. 5; Hab. 1.)

- About one-third of the book of Psalms is composed of psalms of lament.[2]

- There are two types of lament psalms: communal psalms and individual psalms.

- Communal psalms of lament deal with community or national issues or crises. They are a way for God's family to face, feel, and cry out to God concerning their sin or suffering. (See Pss. 44; 60; 74; 79; 80; 83; 89 for examples.)

- There are sixteen community or national psalms of lament and forty-two individual psalms of lament.[3]

- Individual psalms of lament are very similar to communal laments, except they are just between the psalmist and God. (See Pss. 6; 22; 28; 35; 42–43; 88; 102; 109; 142 for examples.)

Lament matters because you matter. What breaks your heart captures God's (Ps. 34:18). So this week we're going to explore the gift of lament—how it can bring you comfort, closeness to God, and health to your soul.

READ PSALM 13 AGAIN, but this time don't stop at verse 4!

In verses 1-4, David described his feelings and perception of reality. When we lament, we do the same; we lay it all out before God. Then, like David, we too move to verse 5. Lament is never a dead end. It's always a stepping stone, an essential step on a path of healing and wholeness. This is why lament can never end at verse 4.

> **Lament is never a dead end. It's always a stepping stone, an essential step on a path of healing and wholeness.**

LOOK AT VERSE 5. David shifted from pouring out his feelings to affirming some choices in verses 5 and 6. List the three choices David made:

1.

2.

3.

We can't always choose our emotions. Sometimes situations press in and bring out all sorts of feelings. But through God's grace, we can control what we do with those feelings. We can let our feelings travel the path of lament in prayer.

Through God's grace, we too can arrive at the choices David did.

We can trust in God's faithfulness, we can rejoice in His character, and we can worship Him.

David closed his psalm with a reason we can make those choices.

What does the end of verse 6 say is the "because," the reason we can make those choices?

David said God has been good to him. The New American Standard Bible (NASB) translation says, "Because He has looked after me." Can you feel the warmth and intimacy of that phrase?

God has been good to you. He has—and He is—looking after you.

My sister, it's OK to lament. God isn't waiting for you to get your emotional act together so you can come to Him with a tidy presentation of trust and rejoicing. No. He has provided the path of lament for you to travel so you can arrive at those choices.

Jesus laments for you, and with you by His Spirit, as we read about in Romans 8. He is wading through the ocean of tears you cry to get to you, attend to you, look after you, and give you a million reasons to trust Him and rejoice.

So let's trust in His unfailing love and sing unto the Lord for He has been good to us!

Amen? Amen!

When You Pray Today

Develop your trust muscle today by praying **Psalm 13:5-6**. Write the verses on a sticky note or type them into your phone and refer to them all day. Affirming those choices in prayer will remind you that **you can trust God** with your pain and it will lead you to a **place of praise**.

Before you begin today's study, pray
PSALM 119:145,

I call with all my heart; answer me, LORD. I will obey your statutes.

DAY TWO

THE ANATOMY OF LAMENT

When I was asked why I wanted to write about lament, my answer was, "Because I believed Melissa Manchester, and it turns out she was wrong."

Are you wondering what I'm talking about? Well, return with me for a moment to my sophomore year of college, to Weyenberg Dorm at Palm Beach Atlantic University, and I'll fill you in.

We're hanging out in the courtyard. I have my keyboard, and we're singing seventies music. Now, if that's not your era, I promise it's still the best decade of music ever, so get your groove on and go with me! I've just finished singing some Lionel Ritchie, and then you say, "Sing 'Don't Cry Out Loud' by Melissa Manchester." So, I start playing those opening chords. I sing it loud and moody with all the angst that song requires, and we all tear up and get wistful because we're all hormonal romantics. But part of the reason I sing it with such conviction is because I believe it.

I used to think it was stoic and strong to keep my feelings to myself and just cry silent tears alone.

But that's not the example of Scripture. David showed us yesterday it's biblical to cry out loud, and this is an example we see repeated throughout Scripture. Crying out to God is the way you worship through prayers of lament. So, let's figure out the framework of lament God set up for us.

> *Lord, thank You for Your Word. Teach us to pray according to Your Spirit and Word. Amen.*

All psalms of lament, whether individual or communal, express loss and longing, trials and trust. While every lament in Scripture is unique, they all follow a general pattern.

READ PSALM 3, PSALM 28, AND PSALM 142.
As you read each psalm, see if you can detect five elements these three psalms share and the general pattern they follow. Pour your coffee or tea and settle in. This is worth a thoughtful read and reflection.

Jot down your observations:

FIVE ELEMENTS

GENERAL PATTERN

NOW LET'S LOOK AT PSALM 3 to reveal the anatomy of lament. What was the psalmist doing in verse 1?

When our prayers of lament begin by addressing God according to His character, they are more likely to end by affirming His worthiness of our praise.

1. EVERY PSALM OF LAMENT BEGINS BY ADDRESSING GOD.

Psalm 3 begins, "LORD." In Psalm 28, David called God his "rock." And in Psalm 142, the psalmist cried out to "the LORD." When we address God in our lamentations, we begin with an understanding of whom we are calling out to. We direct our cries to the One who is all powerful and all good, to the One who is present and attentive. When our prayers of lament begin by addressing God according to His character, they are more likely to end by affirming His worthiness of our praise.

What was the psalmist doing in verse 2?

2. EVERY PSALM OF LAMENT CONTAINS A COMPLAINT OR AN ISSUE BEING TAKEN UP WITH GOD.

Psalm 3's complaint is about the enemies who pursued David. In Psalm 28:3-5, the psalmist complained about injustice and maltreatment. And in Psalm 142:3-4, he lamented endless suffering and feeling like God hadn't come through for him. Later on, we'll figure out how to complain biblically like the psalmists, instead of just whining. But for now, consider that God invites you to process your pain right there with Him.

Think about the truth that God invites you to process your pain with Him. Is that a regular part of your prayer life? Why or why not?

What does that truth reveal to you about God? About the relationship He wants to have with you?

My friend, you're invited to "Cast all your anxiety on [God] because he cares for you" (1 Pet. 5:7, NIV).

Let's keep reading. What was the psalmist doing in Psalm 3:3-6?

3. EVERY PSALM OF LAMENT HAS A POINT WHERE IT TRANSITIONS INTO AN EXPRESSION OF TRUST IN GOD.

For David in Psalm 3, that point happened in verse 3 when he referred to God as his shield. In Psalm 28:6, David affirmed God heard him. In Psalm 142:5, the psalmist confessed God was his refuge. Confessing trust in God is the hinge that turns our grieving into grace, tears into trust, and worries into worship.

What was the psalmist doing in Psalm 3:7?

4. EVERY PSALM OF LAMENT ALSO CONTAINS A REQUEST FOR GOD'S HELP, DELIVERANCE, OR INTERVENTION.

The psalmist uttered the words, "Save me" in verse 7. Psalm 28:2 reads, "Listen to the sound of my pleading," and in Psalm 142:6, the psalmist pleaded, "Rescue me." We're invited to ask God for what we need, desire, and long for.

READ 1 JOHN 5:14. What insight does that verse add to the concept of asking God for what you need?

To me, it bolsters my confidence knowing God is already tuned in, listening for my voice, and ready to act according to His will for me. He really does take care of us, my sister.

OK, last part. What was the psalmist doing in Psalm 3:8?

5. EVERY PSALM OF LAMENT ENDS WITH PRAISE, WORSHIP, OR AFFIRMATION OF GOD'S GOODNESS AND CHARACTER.

Psalm 3:8 ends with David praising God for His salvation. In Psalm 28:6, the psalmist just flat out said, "Blessed be the LORD." And in Psalm 142:7, the psalmist exclaimed that the righteous will gather around him because of God's goodness.

So, let's summarize the five elements of lament psalms. Remember, lament is an important stepping stone on your path of healing. These are not in the exact order of Psalm 3, but you'll see why.

1. **Address God.** (Focus your prayer on the One who hears and answers.)

2. **Pour out your heart.** (Bring Him your complaints and concerns.)

3. **Request help.** (Ask God for what you need.)

4. **Express trust.** (Affirm your faith in His character and His Word.)

5. **Praise Him.** (Worship Him because He is worthy.)

Helpfully, this list forms the acronym APREP. I like to think it's "a prep" so I'm prepared when sorrow or stress show up.

As you study and pray psalms of lament, you'll find those elements in each one, even if the order varies. Sometimes the person who laments expresses trust in God and then requests help; sometimes he calls for help and then expresses trust. The people who prayed those prayers of lament are like you and me, and ultimately they are like Jesus. Scripture tells us Jesus prayed through tears at least twice—in the garden of Gethsemane (Matt. 26; Heb. 5:7) and over the death of Lazarus (John 11:35)—and agonized over Jerusalem (Luke 19:41-44). What an example for us.

Our prayers are often disordered, messy, and vulnerable. That's why God so graciously gave us a path and pattern for our messy emotions to travel in prayer. Letting your tears travel the path of lament will draw you closer to God.

> **Letting your tears travel the path of lament will draw you closer to God.**

Maybe you believed Melissa Manchester like I did. Even if you weren't born when her songs filled the airwaves, have you lived like you can't cry out loud? Or maybe her lyrics describe you right now. If that's you, or was you, do you know why?

> Pause and consider why you're unwilling or unable to cry out to God in honest lament. Don't speed through this, my friend. Take your time. I'll wait! If you need to text or call a trusted friend and talk to her about this, do it.

The reasons you may hesitate to lament can be confusing or complicated. For me, I feared crying out loud was just too messy. I didn't want to complain, be ungrateful, or seem weak. And I didn't want to bother God with my problems.

I thought I was being protective of God. But to be honest, I was being protective of *myself*. I didn't want to feel all sorts of messy emotions I couldn't fix.

It's OK to feel something you can't fix. Lament offers you a safe place to process that pain.

I pray the prayer of Psalm 56:8 (NLT) washes over you with comfort and gives you confidence:

> You keep track of all my sorrows. You have collected all my
>
> tears in your bottle. You have recorded each one in your book.

My friend, God has heard your prayer. Your tears are safe with Him. Celebrate that you are heard and loved and go live like it!

When You Pray Today

Think of a time when your sorrow was so great that you felt it in your throat, and your stress was so palpable that it tightened your chest and rushed your heartbeat. This could have been a personal situation or a communal, national, or world situation that you lament.

Use the **pattern of lament** to create your own prayer with that memory in mind. (Remember APREP.)

AM I JUST COMPLAINING?

Let's start with coffee today, OK? (Or tea, if you're more of a tea girl!) You're in line at Starbucks® and you see me in line ahead of you. You move up in line and say, "Hi," so I ask, "How are you?"

If we have a trusting relationship, you may burst into tears if it's one of those days. If you feel safe with me, you'll be gut-level honest and risk looking weak or confused. You may just throw all the pieces of your broken heart at me knowing I'll show grace, won't judge, and will tenderly care for you. (And then, the barista will give us free drinks just to get us out of there because we're making such a big blubbery scene!)

But if we don't have a trusting relationship and I ask, "How are you?" you'll simply say, "Fine," and take a big gulp of your drink before asking me how I am. A trusting relationship invites honesty.

Through lament, God is inviting an honest conversation based on the question, "How are you?" And if you trust Him, you'll say a whole lot more than "Fine." You'll do what we just did in Starbucks; it's what Psalm 62:8 advises. Before you turn there, pause and ask God to give you discernment as you study.

> *Lord, we need the wisdom of Your Spirit. Teach us how to pour out our hearts to you according to Your Word. Amen.*

NOW, READ PSALM 62:8. What are the two actions included in that verse, and what is the reason we can take those two actions?

In the middle of this psalm, David told us we can trust God and pour our hearts out to Him. We can trust Him at all times and about everything. We can pour out our hearts to Him because He is our safe place.

This sounds great in theory, but when we "pour" it all out to Him, how do we know we aren't just complaining? To know the difference between complaining and lamenting, we need to know the difference between grumbling and groaning.

READ NUMBERS 21:4-5. Circle which words in the following contrasts best represent the Israelites' attitudes and behavior in those verses.

- patient or impatient
- trusting or antagonistic
- humble or demanding
- selfish or surrendered
- grateful or ungrateful

What do those verses suggest about Israel?

The Israelites were world-class grumblers. The posture of grumbling is captured in the phrase they "spoke against God and Moses" (v. 5). That is what grumbling does. It speaks against rather than leaning toward. It pulls back rather than presses in. And the vocabulary of grumbling is clear: "We detest this wretched food!" (v. 5). That "wretched food" was the manna God had provided.

LOOK UP NUMBERS 14:26-30. What was the result of grumbling for the Israelites?

Those who grumbled against God didn't get to enter the promised land. Tough stuff, right? Grumbling doesn't end well. Sin is relational, and so are consequences for sin. Those who grumble show a lack of trust and obedience, and therefore are not allowed to be "with" God in the promised land.

Instead, we groan.

Groaning is the way we express the same ache but from a heart of trust. We pour out our hearts, or tell God our concerns, but with a whole different attitude and posture behind it.

READ PSALM 6:1-3. How do those verses sound different from the passages you read about grumbling?

I hear humility instead of entitlement. Respect rather than resentment. Inquiry rather than accusation. An honest heart groan as the psalmist poured out his feelings to God.

As you read psalms of lament, you'll hear three kinds of groans repeated often. Let's look briefly at each one.

GROAN ONE: PSALMISTS GROANED ABOUT THEIR SIN.

READ PSALM 51:1-15. Think about a regret or a sin in your life. How does Psalm 51 protect you from complaining and show you how to lament instead?

You could have written down a variety of responses to that last question. Among them, David called for mercy, and he owned his sin. He didn't blame or make excuses; he just admitted he was wrong. Those who groan, rather than grumble, take ownership of their sin. They don't blame others, and they humbly ask for forgiveness, knowing "you [God] are right when you pass sentence; you are blameless when you judge" (v. 4).

GROAN TWO: PSALMISTS GROANED ABOUT THEIR ENEMIES.

READ PSALM 35. Think about a situation where you feel opposed, like somebody is out to get you. Or maybe you're facing an antagonistic person. How does David's example in Psalm 35 inform the way you pray about that person or situation? Write down some specific ideas.

If we just grumble about our enemies, we may forget God is the One who avenges. But when we groan to God, like David did, it draws our focus from our enemies to our God. We lift Him higher than our fear or frustration and acknowledge that "He takes pleasure in his servant's well-being" (v. 27).

GROAN THREE: PSALMISTS GROANED ABOUT GOD'S WAYS.

READ PSALM 22. Think about an area in your life where God has allowed something that breaks your heart. Think about God's apparent inaction or action when it comes to that situation. Underline or list a few of the key phrases that distinguish Psalm 22 as an example of lamenting rather than complaining.

Psalm 22:3-5,9-10 helps me hear Psalm 22 as groaning instead of grumbling because the acknowledgment of God's holiness, trustworthiness, and faithfulness are a sacred echo over David's despair. They turn the question, "Why have you forsaken me?" from a tightfisted accusation to an openhanded cry of longing.

Depending on how much of the Bible you've read, the prayer of Psalm 22 may sound familiar to you. It may remind you of another prayer from another's lips in the New Testament.

READ MATTHEW 27:46. How does Jesus's use of this prayer inform the way you relate to God when His ways confuse or hurt you?

Jesus is perfect. Matthew 27:46 shows us how, as He hung on the cross about to die, He cried out to God in lament without complaining. He groaned without grumbling. If Jesus can acknowledge feeling abandoned yet still honor His Father through trust and obedience, so can we. "For he has not despised or abhorred the torment of the oppressed" (Ps. 22:24).

Grumbling is emptying our trash cans. Groaning is emptying our hearts to God.

Grumbling crosses its arms in defiance. Groaning opens its arms in trust.

Grumbling resents God. Groaning runs to God.

Grumbling is an insult to God. Groaning is invited by God and is something God does in and through us, as His Spirit prays for us in our weaknesses with groanings too deep for words.

To finish up, pick **one psalm of lament** and pour out your heart to God along with the psalmist. Be mindful of the difference between grumbling and groaning as you do, and may it draw you even closer to the God who loves you so tenderly. Here are a few ideas if you need help getting started:

- **Psalm 13:** praying through your sadness
- **Psalm 22:** praying through your suffering
- **Psalm 88:** praying through your despair
- **Psalm 137:** praying through your anger

My lament based on Psalm _____:

_____

_____

_____

_____

_____

_____

_____

_____

_____

Amen, and amen. Hear our prayers, Lord.

DAY FOUR
COMMUNAL LAMENT

Before you begin today's study, pray **PSALM 119:145,**

I call with all my heart; answer me, LORD. I will obey your statutes.

It was April 2020, and the world had been shut down for about a month. Every person on every continent was mired in uncertainty, reeling from loss, and most were sheltering in place. Yet it was also the day we celebrated the empty tomb, and I was struck by the empty churches, the empty streets, our empty table, the empty desks in our ministry office, our empty calendars, and so many empty, aching hearts.

So, I sat on our empty couch and turned on the TV. Along with millions of people around the world, I was captivated by the powerful and tender voice of the Italian tenor Andrea Bocelli as it filled my home. But the eerie echo of nothingness outside the Duomo di Milano did me in.

The global icon performed a concert of hope within the walls of the Duomo, and then he stepped outside. On the deserted Piazza del Duomo, Bocelli sang "Amazing Grace." Tears streamed down my cheeks as I felt, not just heard, those words in the midst of a worldwide pandemic. I imagined millions just like me, alone in their homes, joining in harmonious lament.

> Were you there with me that day? What do you remember about that Easter in 2020? How did you grieve the worldwide suffering of the COVID-19 pandemic?

That's what communal lament looks and feels like.

Communal psalms of lament in the Bible deal with local, national, or world issues or crises. They're a way for God's family to face, feel, and cry out to God together concerning their suffering or sin—the ones close to home in the local church and the ones around the world. Today we're going to discover the purpose and power of communal lament.

Lord, thank You for inviting Your family to bring our sorrow to you. Tenderize our hearts as a community to grieve well over our own sin and the sorrow of this world. Amen.

In Psalm 79, the psalmist Asaph captured how I felt during the pandemic in his lament over Israel's exile. (I encourage you to take a few minutes to read the exile backstory in 2 Kings 25.)

As you read Psalm 79, jot down some of the pronouns Asaph used.

The pronouns are collective: *us, we, our.* Asaph wrote a song for all to sing together reflecting their collective sorrows, their shared suffering, and their mutual longings. It's all about "us"!

Let's take a closer look.

Circle the statement that best describes what Asaph did in verses 1-4.

- He set up his case against God.

- He stated the facts of their loss.

Asaph opened by stating the facts that Jerusalem was destroyed, the temple was defiled, and the people were devastated. When we lament as a community, we too spell out the details of our loss or grief.

Now circle which statement best describes what Asaph did in verses 5-7.

- Pleaded for God to turn away His anger.

- Pleaded with God to pour His wrath on the enemy.

Trick question! Both are part of this section of the communal lament. Asaph gave a poetic voice to exiled Israel's longing for God to step in on her behalf. We do that too. As a family, we call out for God to intervene in what seems bigger than us.

Moving on, (circle) which best describes what Asaph did in verses 8-10.

- Called for rescue.

- Created a legal argument.

Asaph gave the community words to call on God for help and rescue. Like Asaph, we can use Scripture to call on God for help and intervention.

Now (circle) which best describes how Asaph finished up in verses 11-13.

- Asked God for provision to rebuild.

- Asked God for mercy for the condemned.

Asaph called the community to plead for those who have no voice—the prisoner, the condemned, those without hope or an advocate. And in humility, Asaph noted that in response to God's deliverance and forgiveness, Israel would praise Him forever. The psalmist called on God to act not for the Israelites' sake but the sake of His great name. Similarly, when we gather as a family to lament, we call on God on behalf of the helpless, and we humbly acknowledge He does all things for His glory.

As God's people, the Israelites gathered to sing with many voices one song expressing their grief, loss, and longing. We need to do the same in our communities of faith. Communal lament in prayer needs to be a regular part of our time together with our brothers and sisters.

Many of the events and situations in our communities, nation, and world should draw us to humble, unified prayer. What are some current events or situations that come to mind that you feel we as God's people should lament together?

Oppression. Injustice. Abuse. Poverty. Prejudice. Division. The list of troubles in our world could go on and on. So, get practical in the way you lament together. Set aside a day to fast and pray with your church or Bible study buddies. Or choose one lament psalm to spend time reflecting on as a community of faith, praying it every day at the same time.

You can also put action to your lament by serving someone who is struggling or suffering, such as partnering with an established ministry serving the underserved or joining with an overlooked person in your community who needs the action of lament to soothe her sorrow and reduce her suffering. Allow your lament to be a pathway of healing for you and those around you.

However, lament is not just a response to suffering; it's also a response to God's Word. Let me show you what I mean.

> **TURN TO DANIEL 9 AND READ VERSES 1-19.** Note the pronouns Daniel also used.

This is a communal lament based on the same subject Asaph lamented in Psalm 79. The suffering of exile prompted Asaph to create his communal lament. But for Daniel, the sin of the exiled people prompted his communal lament.

> **Did you notice what Daniel said in verse 2 before he began this communal lament? What was he reading?**

Daniel was reading Scripture! Specifically, he read Jeremiah's prophecy about this period in Israel's history, from Jeremiah 25.

> **What did Daniel do based on reading God's Word (Dan. 9:3)?**

Daniel turned to God. He pleaded in prayer and lamented. Sure, events prompt lament. Suffering should draw us together to cry out to God as His family. Ultimately, though, lament is a response to the truth of God's Word. The conviction that comes from reading God's Word prompted Daniel to pray.

> **LOOK MORE CLOSELY AT VERSES 5-13.** What did God's Word prompt Daniel to lament?

Though they were suffering and exiled from their land, Daniel voiced a communal lament over Israel's sin. We, the church, need not just lament the suffering we experience and the suffering that surrounds us. We as a church need to lament our own sin.

ALL RIGHT, WE'RE WINDING UP. COMPARE PSALM 79:9 WITH DANIEL 9:18-19. What do these passages have in common?

Both Daniel and Asaph affirm the ultimate purpose of communal lament is "for the glory of your name" (Ps. 79:9) or "for your own sake" (Dan. 9:19).

Sister, we need to lament our sin together. We need to lament suffering together. It is cathartic to pour out your heart with your family of faith. However, we must remember that the point is not our own catharsis. The ultimate purpose of communal lament is to affirm the character of God.

> We, the church, need not just lament the suffering we experience and the suffering that surrounds us. We as a church need to lament our own sin.

When You Pray Today

Join your Bible study sisters in communal lament using Daniel 9 or another psalm of lament. Remember, there is no one way to lament in prayer. Just **let Scripture prompt your words,** and you'll experience the purpose and power of lament.

I'll see you tomorrow for our last day of lament!

Before you begin today's study, pray **PSALM 119:145,**

I call with all my heart; answer me, LORD. I will obey your statutes.

DAY FIVE

LAMENT PREVENTS SOUL CEMENT

My two-year-old Clayton was nestled in his car seat behind me as my friend and I drove to Target. We were listening to an oldies station while little Clayton slung his legs over the arms of his car seat, gnawed on his paci, and watched the passing traffic. He was happy and relaxed until he yelled, "I need!"

I spun around so fast and asked, "What do you need?" I was concerned his little leg was pinched, his diaper had leaked, or who knows what else that could have happened in the back seat. "I need! I need!!!"

So again, I asked, "Clayton, what do you need?"

"I neeeeeeeeed!!!!! I neeeeeeeeeeed!!!!!!"

I checked his diaper and every other possible need and realized the child was just fine. I turned back around and turned up the radio. But for the rest of our drive, he yelled, "I neeeeeeeeeed!" with a giant grin on his cute little face! That silly little guy couldn't name his needs. He didn't know what he was feeling, so he just yelled "I neeeeeeeeed!" on repeat.

Sometimes that's exactly how I feel when I come to God in prayer. I'm full of emotion, but I'm not quite sure what I'm feeling. This reminds me of the psalmist in Psalm 88:1-3:

> LORD, God of my salvation, I cry out before you day and night. May my prayer reach your presence; listen to my cry. For I have had enough troubles, and my life is near Sheol.

Thankfully, the Bible has many great examples that help us learn how to name our feelings and needs in our lament. We'll look at a few together today.

Lord, thank You for including people just like us in Your Word so we can learn and grow. Amen.

FIND AND READ GENESIS 3:10. Note the three distinct parts of Adam's statement after he heard God in the garden:

I was (or felt) _____.

Because I was _____.

So I _____.

Adam named his emotion—*afraid*. He described why he felt that emotion—because he became aware of his nakedness. Then he explained how he acted on that emotion—he hid. Sometimes we don't even know what we're feeling; we just find ourselves hiding and aren't even sure why.

Lament is a way of talking to God that can help you process your emotion and the reasons behind them so you can understand better why you acted as you did.

Adam had to have felt overwhelmed and vulnerable in the garden that fateful day.

BACK UP AND READ GENESIS 3:9-10. Write down what God did (v. 9), and what Adam said in response to God (v. 10).

After Adam and Eve's sin, God went looking for Adam. He didn't leave Adam alone with his sin and shame. Lament is our way of saying, "God, here I am." Don't hide from God if you feel fear, shame, or vulnerability. Don't hide from Him if you've sinned. Come to Him in a prayer of lament and say, "Here I am. This is how I feel, this is where I am, and this is what I've done."

If you feel like Adam, pause and pray Psalm 38 to lament your sin.

On the other hand, think about Hannah. She was suffering, which you already know because you spent time with Hannah and Jackie Hill Perry a couple of sessions ago. Her words in 1 Samuel give us another example of naming our feelings through lament.

How did Hannah explain her lament to Eli the priest in
1 Samuel 1:15-16?

I am (or feel) _____

_____.

I haven't had any wine or beer; I've been _____

_____.

Hannah felt grief, so she poured out her soul to the Lord. She lamented her suffering. If you lament, like Hannah, with a niagara of tears, be comforted because naming those feelings in prayer can keep those feelings from cementing in your soul, making you heavy and stuck.

If you feel like Hannah, pause and pray Psalm 6 to guide your lament.

Adam and Hannah both named their emotions, which is a great reminder for us that naming our emotions is important and healthy. Here's why: When you're feeling intense emotion, like fear or anxiety, the part of your brain that handles "fight or flight" gets fired up. If those emotions overwhelm you, the "fight or flight" can override your more logical thinking. But research has shown that you can actually help that part of your brain chill out by "affect labeling," or naming your emotions.[4]

Lament gives you a place to name your feelings. It is a way for you to worship God with your pain. It is the way to prevent soul cement—getting stuck in your emotions so you can't move forward in your faith.

Never hesitate to be specific in your prayers. Be honest with God about how you feel and what you need.

As we finish, I want you to put this into practice.

READ HABAKKUK 3:17-19. How many times did Habakkuk say "though"?

What word did he use in verse 18 after all those rough "though" scenarios?

Yet, not *but*.

Lament always needs a *yet*, not a *but*. While *but* negates everything that came before it, *yet* indicates inclusion of what was just said with a filter of hope laid on it. *Yet* is the way you acknowledge all those emotions and situations and still move forward in faith.

Lament is like riding a raft down a restless river. You're going somewhere. You feel the tumult and even the refreshment of the experience, and eventually, you reach the shore and the journey ends. Yet the whole time you ride the waves of lament, you're being held, cradled, and drawn by a strong Hand to a safe place.

> Weeping may endure for a night,
>
> But joy comes in the morning.
>
> **PSALM 30:5b (NKJV)**

Just like the sorrow of the cross lasted for a couple of nights, the joy of Christ's new life dawned the morning He walked out of the tomb. The same power that raised Jesus from the dead moves us forward every day (Eph. 1:19-21).

I hope you'll practice lamenting when your heart feels heavy. And I hope you'll practice lamenting to keep your heart light and tender. This world needs women who follow Jesus's example and pray through their pain so their healing can be a balm that comforts others. Be that woman, my friend. Your tears are safe with God.

The same power that raised Jesus from the dead moves us forward every day (Eph. 1:19-21).

Thanks for spending this week with me.

Love,

Jennifer

> Praise be to the God and Father of our Lord Jesus Christ, the
> Father of compassion and the God of all comfort, who comforts
> us in all our troubles, so that we can comfort those in any
> trouble with the comfort we ourselves receive from God.
>
> **2 CORINTHIANS 1:3-4 (NIV)**

When You Pray Today

Take some time now to personalize **Habakkuk 3:17-19** to create your lamentation declaration. I included mine on the next page so you can see what I mean.

MY LAMENTATION DECLARATION

THOUGH _____

_____

THOUGH _____

_____

THOUGH _____

_____

YET _____

_____

GOD IS _____

_____

HE ENABLES ME TO _____

_____

_____

JENNIFER'S LAMENTATION DECLARATION

THOUGH my health fails and I am never healed of blindness,

THOUGH I lose the people I love most and struggle with loneliness,

THOUGH the world spins out of control and life feels crazy at times,

YET I will trust you and keep walking by faith.

GOD IS my strength and hope and life.

HE ENABLES ME TO smile, have joy, and never give up.

WATCH

SESSION FIVE

Watch the Session Five video and take notes below.

TO ACCESS THE VIDEO SESSIONS, USE THE INSTRUCTIONS
IN THE BACK OF YOUR BIBLE STUDY BOOK.

Discuss

If you are part of a *When You Pray* Bible study group, use this page to take notes during your group time and to keep a record of prayer requests that are mentioned.

May You Be Filled

BY JADA EDWARDS

This week we shift our attention to intercessory prayers—the prayers we lift up on behalf of others. The apostle Paul offers numerous intercessory prayers in his New Testament epistles (letters). In fact, his prayers for both individuals and churches often provide great insight to the purpose of his writing and set the tone of his letters. We can learn a lot from him.

The prayer we'll look at this week is the second of two prayers in the book of Ephesians. The first, found in Ephesians 1:15-23, is Paul's prayer that these believers would have divine *sight*. Then, in Ephesians 3:14-21, he prayed for their divine *strength*. These are complementary prayers. Paul wanted the Ephesians to learn who they were and what they had in Christ and then live accordingly. So that's how he asked God to act in their lives and their church.

As we walk through Paul's prayer for the Ephesian Christians, the purpose for his prayer becomes clear: Paul's pastoral heart was heavy for the health of this church, and it is expressed with a passionate plea for supernatural love and unity from a more than able God.

BIBLE PASSAGE
Ephesians 3:14-21

PRAYER TYPE
Prayers of Intercession

I pray that you, being rooted and firmly established in love, may be able to comprehend with all the saints what is the length and width, height and depth of God's love.

EPHESIANS 3:17b-18

DAY ONE
REMEMBER YOU HAVE THE SAME FATHER

TO BEGIN, READ EPHESIANS 3:14-21.

I am not a fan of icebreakers and team building. My philosophy is to *let me break the ice in my own time and in my own way.* And when it comes to teams? I'll do the selecting, thank you very much! That's the transparent truth for me as a mostly extroverted, selectively-introverted, debater, achiever-with-a-bent-toward-individualism.

I say all that to make clear the pain I endured when I recently participated in an icebreaker activity in a room I was hoping to slip out of early. Instead, I found myself submitting to the authority of the facilitator and talking to people I had never met until we found a decidedly unique thing in common. I talked and talked, introduced and reintroduced. Eventually, I did find someone who had an eerily similar family structure to mine. Like me, her father was raised by a single dad who later married (introducing a stepmother into the family) and ultimately died at a young age. Shortly after his death, the stepmother remarried, creating a household of children (including our fathers) raised by their stepmother and her husband. Strange, right? I know. The point is, I had never met someone who shared that heritage, and so as a reward for my participation, the Lord blessed me with a special connection that day.

> What about you? Are there people with whom you struggle to connect? If so, why do you think that is? If not, what have you learned over time to help make this easier for you?

My memory of that awkward but rewarding icebreaker moment often surfaces when I need to be reminded of how God can create connection however and wherever He wants. Keep that in mind as we begin to unpack Paul's prayer for the Ephesian church today.

READ ALL OF PAUL'S PRAYER IN EPHESIANS 3:14-21 AGAIN.

Before we get too far into Paul's words, I think it will help us to make sure we understand what intercessory prayer is and why it's an important category of our prayers. We've already learned about prayers of petition, which we defined as "a prayer requesting something of a deity" (see p. 50).[1] That's essentially what intercession is, except it's petitioning God on behalf of others. You may have grown up in a church that had prayer "intercessors," or maybe you heard people refer to "interceding" for someone. Those words are related and connected to the type of prayer we are studying this week.

LOOK UP THE FOLLOWING VERSES. Next to each one, write down who was the one praying, who was being prayed for, and a one-word description of the request being made.

	Who was the one praying?	Who was being prayed for?	What request was made?
Luke 22:32			
John 17:8-9			
John 17:20-21			

From these examples, what are some general conclusions you can make about intercessory prayer? How do you know it makes a difference?

We pray for others because that's what Jesus did. Time and again the Gospels show Jesus making requests of God the Father on behalf of others, and He continues to do that even now from His place at the right hand of God (Heb. 7:25). As His followers, this is an important part of our ministry, too (1 Tim. 2:1). But what does it look like? I'm glad you asked!

REREAD EPHESIANS 3:14.

Paul opened his prayer for the Ephesian believers with the phrase, "For this reason." What reason was Paul referencing? There are a few different ideas on this because what immediately precedes this phrase is a long detour in Ephesians 3:2-12, which concludes with Paul reminding them to stay encouraged. I believe the "reason" for Paul's prayer has to do with the weighty things he shared with his readers in 2:1–3:1.

GO BACK AND READ EPHESIANS 2:1-10. What phrases or words stand out in these verses? What do they mean to you?

You could have chosen a variety of words to summarize Paul's point in verses 1-10, but I imagine the word you picked had something to do with change, transformation, salvation, grace, or the gospel. Think about the gravity of what Paul revealed here. You were dead in your trespasses and sins; you were walking in darkness, and your heritage was disobedience. But God, being rich in mercy, made you alive together with Christ, through no work or effort of your own, but simply because He is merciful.

Being alive with Christ means you're raised up with Him and seated with Him in the heavenly places (v. 6). You've been saved by grace through faith; therefore, Christ expects good work out of you (vv. 8,10). In the next set of verses, he unpacked what it means to be God's new "workmanship."

NOW READ EPHESIANS 2:11-22. Again, what phrases or words stand out in these verses? What do they mean to you?

Did you go with *hope*, *rescue*, *gratitude*, or something along those lines? Paul wrote this letter to a church in a bustling city at a time when the gospel was just beginning to spread out from the Jewish people to the Gentiles, of which there were many in Ephesus. In case you're wondering if the gospel message affected the generations of cultural and ethnic division between Jews and Gentiles, the answer is a resounding yes. This is why Paul's words to the church were so important.

> **READ BACK OVER EPHESIANS 2:13-20** and really let those words sink in.

Friend, that's not just a mouthful; it's a head-full and heart-full. God saves us from sin so we can be reconciled to Him and to one another. Despite how miraculous that notion is, it's not an easy one to live out. Even the most grateful heart and willing spirit will struggle to constantly pursue unity, reconciliation, and love—especially when it's easier to stay in our original camps and love selectively from a distance.

So, how do we do this? Like Paul, we make praying for others a priority in our personal prayers and the prayer habits of our churches. We do that not just by knowing Scripture but by asking God for specific directions for those we pray for.

> **READ EPHESIANS 3:14-15.** What stands out to you from the beginning of Paul's prayer? What do you make of Paul's posture? Of his choice of words?

At the beginning of the prayer in Ephesians 3, Paul made it clear to his audience that we have one Father. For Jews and Gentiles, the importance of being one family can't be overlooked or understated. To be clear, *Gentiles* is a broad term used to describe anyone who is not a Jew. Hello, my name is Jada, and I'm a Gentile.

The differences between Jews and Gentiles could be seen in the foods they ate, how they dressed, and certainly in how they worshiped. They differed in their approach to academics, education, and the arts. They had conflicting ideas of righteousness, rules for living, and the list goes on. Jews and Gentiles weren't peer groups in the culture of that day. There was active hostility fed by prejudice. Jews clearly saw themselves in the position of privilege, which had as much to do with birthright as it did an individual's standard of right living (obedience to the law). This issue is one Paul addressed often, particularly in Galatians and Romans.

For hundreds of years, we Gentiles were far from the Lord. God had given the Jewish people special access to Himself. From Abraham in Genesis 12, God set them apart as chosen with the intention of having a people to reflect His glory to the nations, and for generations, the gap between Jews and Gentiles remained strong. Then the promised

Messiah came—the Savior of the Jewish people. Where the people of Israel failed to be the light to the nations they were called to be, Jesus fulfilled. He established His church and desires that it is defined by unity and love (John 17:21) and available to "all nations" (Matt. 28:19). This is the "mystery" Paul spoke of in Ephesians 3:4-6. Jesus Christ demolished the power of geography, labels, prejudice, traditions, and rules through His unifying grace—and that was always His plan.

> **When you truly understand the weight of Christ's work in tearing down division, what changes in the way you view other people?**

The kind of reconciliation we're talking about goes beyond finding a few things in common, shopping at the same store, or showing kindness. This is being made into a *new family*—even "one body" (Eph. 2:16)—where you share the name of Christ and redemption is the connection. The word for "family" Paul used in his prayer (3:15) is *patria*, and it means "people of successive generations who are related by birth."[2] In Christ we have a new heritage and one Father who seeks our good and sees us as sons and daughters and brothers and sisters. For the Jews of Paul's day, many of whom held their lineage and families in high regard, this meant everyone was in need of the saving grace of Jesus. No one had a right to look down on anyone else. For Gentiles, often seen as second-class citizens, this meant they had no reason to feel less than anyone else. Christ created a new family that anyone can be a part of.

> Christ created a new family that anyone can be a part of.

When I consider the beautiful mystery of this, I'm encouraged and hopeful. This prayer is so relevant for us today because across the globe, countries and regions suffer from the poisonous effects of racism, classicism, sexism, and other prejudices that prevent harmony. Of course, in America, I live this and see it firsthand. So, at the very least, I can understand the struggle between the Jews and the Gentiles to live in this new way. In reality, I more than understand; I empathize. To unravel the intricate threads of ethnic and cultural division is no easy task. If we can't grasp what Christ did at the macro level between Jews and Gentiles, we'll never be able to be "family" at the micro level with our neighbors.

This means I must keep my bias in front of me. It means I must be willing to admit that despite the sacrificial work of Christ, I won't always be inclined toward unity and harmony. And it means this language of unity needs to be at the forefront of how I pray for others.

I wonder how my choices would change if I saw everyone as a favorite brother or sister, a favorite aunt or uncle, or that close cousin who becomes my lifelong friend. What if I imagine the person I'm in conflict or disagreement with, or deeply offended by, as someone sitting next to me at our Father's table? Would I have more grace and patience? Could I disagree with love? Would I be more willing to stay at the table and not as quick to walk away or dismiss?

I can tell you the answer is yes. Yes, I would choose to stay. Yes, I would pray before I respond. Yes, I would be quicker to apologize and accept the apologies of others. And beyond that, the way I pray for people—interceding for their needs, their salvation, their relationships with the Lord—would grow to look more like Jesus.

> READ EPHESIANS 3:14-15 ONE MORE TIME. Write down one way this passage challenges you to pray for others.

As the backdrop of this passionate pastoral prayer, Paul wanted us to remember we are one family with the same Father with the same Father, and that's a stronger bond than having things in common with one another. I encourage you to keep in mind that we have no grounds for hostility toward one another, even when we passionately disagree, because of the work of Christ. I challenge you to ask God for clarity to see your own pain and tendencies in light of His deep desire for unity in His body. And I invite you to ask for that same clarity as you intercede for others. A perspective of unity can significantly change how we pray with the same Father, and that's a stronger bond than having things in common with one another.

When You Pray Today

Take some time to sit honestly before the Lord. Ask Him to show you where you need to live in unity with others if it's not already obvious. Then, pick one relationship or group of people to intercede for today and begin your prayer with the words of Ephesians 3:14-15.

DAY TWO
AN UNLIMITED SUPPLY OF STRENGTH

It's hard to imagine now, but there was a time before fire hydrants in which firefighters had to carry buckets of water to a fire. "These bucket brigades were the best system we had [for putting out fires.] Firefighters stood in a line between the fire and the source of water and passed buckets along, one by one until the fire was extinguished," or they would drive tanks of water to the fire and carry water by the bucket.[3] Then, in the early 1800s came the invention of the fire hydrant. It was a game changer because it was a direct connection to a town or city's water source.

This image of connection to the source is what I see when I think about the part of Paul's prayer for the Ephesian Christians that we will take a look at today.

> **READ EPHESIANS 3:14-16.** Write verse 16 in the space below. Circle each pronoun "his." Underline the noun that follows each "his."

> Verse 16 contains the first request of Paul's prayer. What one word or idea sums it up?

Before you begin today's study, pray **PSALM 119:135,**

Make your face shine on your servant, and teach me your statutes.

Yesterday, we saw how Paul's intercessory prayer for the Ephesians began by appealing to God the Father and reminding the Ephesians that in Christ we are all one family. With verse 16, Paul brought his first request before God—that the Ephesians receive the strength or power of the Holy Spirit.

More specifically, Paul prayed that they be strengthened "according to the riches of [God's] glory." The phrase *according to* means "in harmony with," which is not the same as "out of."[4] Paul didn't ask for a measure of power from God's perfect glory; He asked for power in proportion to God's glory.

Not just a portion but in proportion. Try and wrap your mind around that. This prayer is for strength that is in line with God's abundance rather than our lack, and God's ability instead of our limitations.

TAKE A MOMENT TO READ EPHESIANS 1 for a glimpse at the expanse of God's glory and the overflow of that glory to His creation. Do you pray for God to fix a certain situation a specific way (portion), or do you pray for God to show up in the way He wants (proportion)?

The glory of God is the sum total and brilliance of all His attributes. Because God Himself is infinite and eternal (remember our study of Ps. 139?), His glory is inexhaustible (see also Ex. 33:18-20; Ps. 19:1-4). The strength of God in us isn't finite because God's glory isn't finite. There's no cutoff or allotment that we are unable to exceed. There's no measure of strength for a certain day or time frame. Instead, there is a river of strength that flows to us out of God's infinite ocean of glory. This is the living presence of God in us by His Spirit. The more we need from moment to moment, the more is available. This idea brings tears to my eyes, chills to my skin, and courage to my soul. I can know with blessed assurance that I have enough strength for any given task ahead. I can come to terms with the fact that in my brokenness and weakness and unworthiness, God chose me, by His grace and my faith, as a vessel for His power.

What is a situation or relationship where you need to be reminded of the strength and power of the Holy Spirit available to you today?

What are some things or people you have been looking to for strength instead of the Lord?

Do you find yourself relying on your knowledge instead of yielding to the Spirit? Are you tempted to see your spiritual activity as the source of your strength?

This strength isn't in proportion to your behavior or the version of yourself that you show others. It isn't based on your kindness, church attendance, or volunteer service. It doesn't matter how generous or patient you think you are. Those things are all great, but they can't strengthen you for the life God intends for you to live. On my best day, I am still sinful and prideful, and that taints even my most focused efforts. I desperately need the Spirit, who is God, to be my internal, infinite supply of strength.

Paul prayed that this strength be manifested in our "inner man" or "inner being." We aren't saved by our "outer man"; therefore, we won't be sanctified, or grow in holiness, by the outer man either. The inner man is where we meet God, and we are changed. It is where God redeems and where He most wants to work. We rely on the Spirit of God, promised by Jesus, to guide us in wisdom and give us strength. When we yield to the guidance of the Spirit, we gain access to the strength available only in Him.

In light of that, I nourish my soul with the Word of God—this is the tool of the Spirit. His job is to illuminate and bring to mind the teaching of Jesus (John 14:17) so I apply it with wisdom. The Spirit leads me in what to do and gives me strength to do it! It really doesn't get better than that.

Do you struggle to feel assured God will give you strength for the mission He's called you to and everything you're facing? Write Ephesians 3:16 on a note card to carry with you or place it somewhere you'll see it often and be reminded of the strength of the Spirit in you.

It's time to unpack those feelings of powerlessness. When you feel unable to live in a way that pleases God, you need to pause and walk in power. Some of you are thinking "Jada, you just oversimplified that!" Listen, you already know where the enemy and your own flesh try to trip you up. Are you easily offended and looking for justification to hold a grudge (no matter how small)? Maybe you wrestle with taking steps of faith because you really, really, really would like everything to be planned out, with a backup plan, and all the necessary resources identified and available. It could be that you're struggling with a habit of pleasure, dependence, or indulgence, and it's difficult to tell yourself no. You could be haunted by trauma or a deep pain that made you feel powerless.

> Do any of those sound like you today? What do you sense God calling you to let go of in order to make room for the Spirit to work?

Even when our physical, emotional, or intellectual power fails us, our spiritual power does not. This simple truth is foundational to our prayer lives because if you aren't convinced of your power (through the Spirit), you can't understand the impact of intercessory prayer. When we pray for others, it's more than just wishful thinking. Remember that fire hydrant image? You're always connected to the Source—the Holy Spirit and His power. We pray with God-given power, and we have assurance that He absolutely will demonstrate His power in the lives of those we pray for. So, pray daily to be strengthened with His power. Pray daily for others to be strengthened by His power, following the example Paul gives us here. And by all means, ask others to pray this for you, too.

Paul's failures fueled his passion to pray for the church, and the same should be true for us.

Loving Jesus is easy. Living like you love Jesus is no joke (that's the understatement of the century). Life is unfair. But I have good news. No, it's not a magic formula to remove all struggling and erase hard times. This news is even better. It's the promise for every believer. The Holy Spirit empowers you for every circumstance, and He empowers you as you pray in every circumstance—not just for yourself but for others. When the fatigue of simply living life hits you, sometimes it's a reminder that we're all subject to the challenges of this life. May you be compelled to think beyond yourself and remember you have power to cover someone else. As a matter of fact, God often uses our own crazy life situations to give us insight and compassion as we cover others. Paul knew what it was like to walk in his own power and live for his own glory. His failures fueled his passion to pray for the church, and the same should be true for us.

Take time (whether in a moment or for a few days) to reset and realign. Do that by pausing and remembering you have power. You're not the source of it; you're the steward of it. Steward it well and with the confidence that it's always accessible—to you personally and as a tool for intercessory prayer. As you pray for others, remember times in your own life where you struggled. Then, you can pray specifically and with empathy. Don't let the enemy lie and tell you you're powerless (or clueless). He wants you to try and win God's favor as opposed to realizing you already have it! Resist the enemy and "be strengthened with power in your inner being through his Spirit" (Eph. 3:16).

READ EPHESIANS 3:16 ONE MORE TIME. Write down one way this verse challenges you to pray for others.

When You Pray Today

As you pray, ask God to **renew your sense of awe** and remind you of His power.

As you pray for yourself or reflect on your life, ask God to bring to your heart those who may be having similar struggles to you and **cover them in prayer.**

If God has already put someone on your heart to pray for, ask Him to show you how your own story creates a path of compassion and understanding for that person. At the intersection of **power** and **compassion** is **life-changing prayer.**

WHERE CHRIST LIVES, THERE MUST BE LOVE

Before you begin today's study, pray **PSALM 119:135,**

Make your face shine on your servant, and teach me your statutes.

Once upon my career, I used to travel out-of-state frequently. For three years I traveled back and forth every couple of weeks to Seattle. Three weeks there, one week home. Interestingly, about a month before I took the traveling assignment, I purchased a condo. I was excited and felt like a real adult. But I remember a friend coming to visit one day and looking around the condo with a look of confusion. I asked what was wrong, and she said, "I thought you said you live here."

"I do!" I said. "Why would you say that?"

She said, "I don't think you really live here." I looked at her like she was crazy (that's what real friends do). She paused and then started asking questions about my neighborhood. "What's your favorite place to eat? What's the best dry cleaners? Where's the nearest park?"

Guess what? I didn't have a good answer for any of her questions. Because although I paid the mortgage each month, my life wasn't there. I had an address, but I didn't abide there.

BEGIN BY READING EPHESIANS 3:14-19.

Another word for *abide* is *dwell*, and it's the foundation of today's portion of Paul's prayer—verses 17-19. These verses build on the previous ones; it's the first result, or "so that," Paul expressed will come from the inner power we have through the Spirit according to the riches of God's glory. He also affirmed the "reason" mentioned in verse 14 is a call back to chapter 2.

READ THE FIRST HALF OF VERSE 17 AGAIN. THEN, READ EPHESIANS 2:21-22. What word jumps out at you from both of these passages of Scripture?

In Ephesians 2:22 and 3:17, Paul used a version of the word *dwell*, which means "to settle down and abide or to take up permanent abode."[5] As used by Paul, this word refers to the possession of a human being by God.

From the very beginning in the garden, God has desired to dwell in and among His people. In the Old Testament, this was the purpose of the tabernacle in the wilderness and the temple in Jerusalem. In the New Testament, we see this first in Jesus, Immanuel—God with us—and then in the Holy Spirit, who dwells in every believer (1 Cor. 12:13). In Isaiah 57:15 we read:

> For the High and Exalted One, who lives forever, whose name is holy, says this: "I live in a high and holy place, and with the oppressed and lowly of spirit, to revive the spirit of the lowly and revive the heart of the oppressed."

Each believer, and therefore the church, is a dwelling place of God in the Spirit. With the power of the Trinity in mind (Father, Eph. 3:14; Spirit, v. 16; Son, v. 17), Paul prayed that Christ dwells in us as it was intended. More than casual encounters or the practice of inviting Christ in times of crisis, we should make room for Christ to permanently reside within us. So, how exactly do we make room? By faith.

Similar to verse 16's mention of the inner self, we again see reference to the nature rather than the behavior with the phrase "in your hearts." In the innermost sanctuary of your being, Christ is to be given the place of preeminence. Remember, this is a prayer Paul prayed for Ephesian Christians, so this is not about salvation but about Christ dwelling in the believer for the purpose of sanctification (the ongoing work of being freed from sin or becoming more holy).

Ephesians 3:17 "is the only place in Scripture that specifically mentions Christ dwelling in our hearts," but it expresses the sentiment of Jesus in John 15:4-5 (ESV).[6]

> Abide in me, and I in you. As the branch cannot bear fruit by itself, unless it abides in the vine, neither can you, unless you abide in me. I am the vine; you are the branches. Whoever abides in me and I in him, he it is that bears much fruit, for apart from me you can do nothing.

Two times Jesus commanded us to allow Him to abide, or remain, in us. We know that we must abide in Him, but the reverse is true as well. To help this make sense, I think about the idea of a child who lives in the home of her parents. She abides or dwells there. But also, as she grows, she can choose to allow her parents' teaching and values to abide or dwell in her. She abides in their home, and her heart becomes a home for their instruction. She becomes a product of her parents—by choice. So, the parents choose to have a child in their home, as Christ has chosen us. But the child chooses to hold fast to the words of her parents, as we must choose to hold dear and be led by the word of Christ.

> What are some ways you daily choose to be led by the word of Christ? Can you think of an example from yesterday?

> Instead of praying for God to heal, fix or bless others, have you thought about asking that Christ richly dwell in their hearts? (It's easy to choose felt need over being filled with Christ.)

> **NOW READ EPHESIANS 3:17-19 AGAIN.**

When we hold fast to the word of Christ, we anchor ourselves in Him, and the result is we are rooted in love. Being rooted and grounded in love is clearly connected to inviting Christ to dwell in our hearts. If Christ is truly living in us and through us, our lives must be defined by love.

Paul used both agricultural (rooted) and architectural (grounded) metaphors. He wanted to paint a picture of depth and foundation. To be rooted in love reminds me of the tree planted by its water source and bearing fruit in Psalm 1:3. It is strong and fruitful and has roots that allow it to survive and even grow in drought and unpredictable storms. Being grounded in love reminds me of the firm foundation required to sustain any structure. Jesus used similar imagery in Matthew 7:24-27.

> **READ PSALM 1:1-3 AND MATTHEW 7:24-27.** What is the Christian to be rooted in, according to these verses?

What is the Christian to be rooted in according to Paul in Ephesians 3:17-18?

Was Paul describing something entirely different from the psalmist and Jesus? How would you describe the relationship between God's Word and God's love?

When we have a solid foundation in God's love, which we gain from the study of His Word, we can better understand the "breadth and length and height and depth" of it (v. 18, ESV). And based on Romans 8:38-39, " . . . neither death nor life, nor angels nor rulers, nor things present nor things to come, nor powers, nor height nor depth, nor any other created thing will be able to separate us from the love of God, which is in Christ Jesus our Lord."

Paul desperately wanted the Ephesians to grasp the love of Jesus, and it was at the heart of His prayer for them. Being rooted in love shows up in the way we love God and people. The entire law is summed up with these two commandments (Matt. 22:37-39). This kind of love is beyond affection, and it's bigger than a personality type. Love is the identifying character trait of those who follow Jesus (John 13:35) because love is who our God is (1 John 3–4). When Christ dwells in our hearts, we are so grounded in love that we are able to see people in the image of God. This type of love should be something we daily ask God to manifest in us and something we daily pray for others in the spirit of Paul's prayer.

Where do you struggle to love well? Do some people seem harder to love?

> Love is the identifying character trait of those who follow Jesus (John 13:35) because love is who our God is (1 John 3–4).

How have your past understandings or experiences shaped your ideas about love? Is love the lens through which you try to see others and life?

What impact does this have on your readiness to pray for others or the specific ways in which you do?

Regardless of how we start in life, loving people God's way will take some work. If you had a wonderful childhood and healthy, Christian family, there will be people who are difficult for you to love because you don't understand them and/or were never exposed to them. If you experienced unhealthy, distorted, or abusive behaviors labeled as "love," it won't be simple to switch and understand the depth and breadth of God's love. This is why it's so important to start with Christ as the definition of love (1 John 4:10), to invite Him to dwell in your heart, and for you to dwell in His Word. Only the Spirit of God can heal you from wrong or limited views of love and lead you in God's idea of love.

Paul desires that this church is not merely satisfied with being rescued and redeemed by Christ. He desires that Jesus reside in their hearts. Paul knows this "residence" results in Christlike love, even when it's difficult and inconvenient. Christlike love shows up in our actions and choices. When we choose to pray for others, we must be careful that it's driven by love for them. That means we aren't just praying for things that benefit us (*Lord, please change my friend, my spouse, my kids, and so forth*). We're praying for what God desires for them. That is an expression of real love.

Do the work of establishing a thorough understanding of God's idea of love. In 1 Corinthians 13, we see a full picture of what God's love should look like through us. But here's the challenge, those verses aren't to be reduced to a checklist in order that we behave better. They are the evidence of Christ dwelling deep in our hearts and grounding us in love.

READ 1 CORINTHIANS 13. Summarize this picture of God's love.

When I think about the power of God's love, I become acutely aware of how conditional my love can be. I realize that God's love is steadfast and enduring, but mine gives up too easily. I see that God's love is patient and kind, but mine can be either too passive or too aggressive. Can anybody out there relate?

Remember, the goal isn't to try harder to be more loving. The goal is to be more yielding, more surrendered to Christ so that when He dwells in us more, love is the evidence of His presence, not the effort of our work. And that love allows us to pray insightful and intercessory prayers for others.

> **READ EPHESIANS 3:17-19 ONE MORE TIME.** Write down one way these verses challenge you to pray for others.

When You Pray Today

How can you make more space for Christ to dwell in your heart? What areas are you holding back? As you continue to surrender more to Christ, He dwells more richly in you, and you can live out His love. Today, ask God to show you how to **pray loving prayers even if they're uncomfortable and unpopular**. Don't just say yes to those who seem easy to love. Choose to intercede for someone who may be hard for you to love but needs your intercession.

Before you begin today's study, pray **PSALM 119:135,**

Make your face shine on your servant, and teach me your statutes.

DAY FOUR

GOD'S ABILITY WILL EQUIP YOU FOR HIS WORK

I remember applying for scholarships for college. There were several criteria I had to meet. A particular grade point average, involvement in extracurricular activities, demonstration of leadership ability, and more. I did manage to receive a few small scholarships (don't be too impressed), and I was grateful. The thing about those scholarships is that the giving organizations often had large amounts of money to give, but they didn't give it to just anybody who asked. They gave to certain people for certain purposes. Those organizations want to make their names known, and they want to earn goodwill in the community and in the marketplace. Their goodwill is for their "glory."

The same is true of God. He has given every believer the power of the Holy Spirit, but His "criteria" is that we use that power for the Father's purposes. God's lavish grace is more than random blessings for our personal agendas; His goodwill is so His glory might be displayed in our lives. Let's look at the next portion of Paul's prayer to understand this more.

READ ALL OF PAUL'S PRAYER IN EPHESIANS 3:14-21.

The close of Paul's prayer in Ephesians 3:20-21 is often referred to as a doxology, which is a statement of praise to God. Paul's reflection on the power of God at work in the life of the believer and the unity of the church led Paul to this prayer of worship and praise. Today we'll consider verse 20, and tomorrow we'll end our week with verse 21.

As we near the conclusion of Paul's prayer, we encounter a very popular, often-quoted verse:

Now to him who is able to do above and beyond all that we ask or think according to the power that works in us.

EPHESIANS 3:20

Fill in the blanks with what Ephesians 3:20 reveals about:

God ("him"): _____

The Christ-follower (us): _____

Paul praised God for His divine attributes of authority (also known as sovereignty) and power (or omnipotence). God controls all things, and He has the power to do anything. Greek scholar Kenneth Wuest says, "the compound word is a superlative of superlatives in force. It speaks of the ability of God to do something, that ability having more than enough potential power, this power exhaustless, and then some on top of that. Thus, Paul says that God is able to do super-abundantly above and beyond what we ask or think, and then some on top of that."[7]

Think of it like this: *God cannot give us more than He is (because He is inexhaustible), but He can give us so much more than we are.* However, this powerful certainty is often used out of context. Let's think about where we are in Paul's prayer and apply this truth.

> Was this part of Paul's prayer familiar to you before this study? Have you ever used or heard this verse used out of context?

A popular way to use this verse is to arbitrarily declare God's ability to work in our favor and on our behalf. But it is actually a conclusive statement to Paul's prayer, as indicated by the word, *Now*. If it's a conclusion, we must be clear on what precedes it. Summarizing from verses 14-19, Paul has prayed on behalf of the Ephesians that they are: 1) pursuing unity as one family; 2) living in the power of the Holy Spirit; 3) inviting Christ to dwell in their hearts; 4) being grounded in love; and 5) being filled by God with His own fullness. Then, with this spiritual alignment, they can declare and invite God's inexhaustible and unimaginable ability which, by the way, they need if they're going to live holy.

When those conditions aren't our foremost passion and pursuit, we should know that God's work in us is limited. Romans 8:28 echoes the same principle (emphasis added):

> We know that all things work together for the good of those who love God, who are called according to *his* purpose.

Yes, God works everything out; but, like those scholarship organizations, it's for a certain reason and for certain people—*for His purpose* and *for those who love Him*. There is no limitation in His ability, and therefore there is no limit to what God can do in and through us.

Keeping all of this in mind, paraphrase Ephesians 3:20.

God desires that the greatness of His ability be displayed through us. This is the promise Jesus told His disciples:

> Truly I tell you, the one who believes in me will also do the works
> that I do. And he will do even greater works than these, because
> I am going to the Father. Whatever you ask in my name, I will
> do it so that the Father may be glorified in the Son. If you ask me
> anything in my name, I will do it.
>
> JOHN 14:12-14

God is without a doubt able to do far beyond what we can even know to ask, but His ability will only go toward advancing His agenda. So often we establish agendas for our lives and then invite God in when we've reached the end of ourselves or when we've hit a crisis we can't manage. This verse can become like the saved passwords we don't think about anymore because they autopopulate. We visit our favorite websites and use our favorite apps, but how many times do we know our actual password? Once it's saved on our devices, we don't think about it anymore, but we want it to grant us access when needed. That's nice for passwords that we struggle to remember, but God's Word doesn't work that way. Scripture is more than magic phrases we casually call out and expect God to act upon. We need to be more concerned about how God's plan is going forward than we are about our plan going forward.

In a society obsessively focused on "#goals," we must modify that to be focused on "#Godsgoals." His abundant ability is exclusively for His agenda, and we have the privilege of partnering with Him to achieve our portion of it.

There's one more feature of this prayer I don't want you to miss. Verse 20 is not actually asking God to do anything; it is declaring who He is. Are you catching on to this pattern in the prayers of the Bible? Paul didn't say, "Now, God, based

In a society obsessively focused on "#goals," we must modify that to be focused on "#Godsgoals." His abundant ability is exclusively for His agenda, and we have the privilege of partnering with Him to achieve our portion of it.

on your unfathomable ability, could you start blessing my life?" Paul concluded his prayer with praise to the Father for His divine attributes, an aspect of prayer we've seen from Jesus in the Lord's Prayer, Hannah in 1 Samuel 2, David in Psalm 139, and the psalmists who find reasons to praise God even in their lament. Paul wrapped up his intercessory prayer for the church at Ephesus with praise—adoration and acknowledgment of who God is and the reminder that the God we seek to love is able to help us love Him.

Where do you need reassurance of God's abundant ability?

How often do you spend time in prayer declaring to God who He is?

We should be comforted by the power and ability of our God. We should pray according to that power and pray that power is displayed in our lives according to God's plan. How blessed we are that God is omniscient and omnipotent—all-knowing and all-powerful. When God is not moving in the way we want, it's not for lack of ability; it's because He has a different agenda. That doesn't mean that what we want isn't good sometimes. There's nothing wrong with wanting marriage, healing, career advancement, healthy kids, or financial comfort. But there is something wrong when 1) those things become our primary goals, and 2) we are uninterested in God's goals. The thing I want from God can easily become my god. If I'm not careful, I'll find myself asking God to use His power and ability to keep an idol on the throne of my life. I have to seek God's agenda before I call on His ability, and that's hard to do in an isolated moment if it has not been a consistent pursuit in my life.

TAKE A FEW MINUTES TO READ 2 CORINTHIANS 3:1-6; 4:1-6 AND THEN READ EPHESIANS 1:10. From these passages of Scripture, what do you learn about God's agenda?

God's agenda is clearly communicated to us in His Word, which means it never changes. He desires to transform His children into the image of Christ (2 Cor. 3–4) and to unite all things to Christ (Eph. 1:10). As Jesus put it, He came "to seek [unite to Him] and to save [transform] the lost" (Luke 19:10).

> **READ EPHESIANS 3:20 ONE MORE TIME.** Write down one way this verse challenges you to pray for others.

When You Pray Today

What are some ways you can ask God to display His power in exceeding abundance? Here are three important areas you can stretch your faith and pray for God's power to be more evident.

1. **In your personal life.** Ask God for power that shows up in practical ways. Do you need God's power to forgive or mend a relationship? Do you need God's power for your contentment while you wait? Maybe you need it so that your joy is consistent and not conditional.

2. **In the lives of others.** Whether strangers God brings across your path or family and friends, how can you specifically pray for God's power in someone's life? Emotional healing? Financial need? Faith to live on mission?

3. **In the church.** Ask God for His power in helping your local church and in the global church. We need to love with God's power, speak with His power, and serve with His power. The world needs the hope that the church has, but the church needs to walk more boldly in God's power.

DAY FIVE
A CANVAS FOR GOD'S GLORY

Before you begin today's study, pray **PSALM 119:135,**

My friend is an amazing artist. She sees every blank surface as an opportunity. Where there is a blank wall or a blank canvas, her mind instantly sees a place to bring to life what's in her heart and mind. God sees us the same way. The individual believer and the church are canvases for God's glory to be displayed. All of His abundance and love is to be shown through our lives. Keep this visual in mind as we bring Paul's prayer for the Ephesian church to a close.

> **READ EPHESIANS 3:14-21 ONE MORE TIME.** Then, read Ephesians 3:20-21 aloud (if you're somewhere you can get away with it).

Paul closed his intercessory prayer with this lofty picture of the church because the main point he'd been explaining to them is "how the church is God's new creation, brought into existence by the cross that broke down the barrier between Jews and Gentiles."[8] God's glory is displayed in His church when we live like who we are in Christ.

Listen to how the church is described in God's Word: The church is established by Jesus and protected from being defeated by the gates of Hades (Matt. 16:18). Jesus loves His church so fully that husbands are to love their wives in the same way (Eph. 5:25). It is "the general assembly and church of the firstborn" (Heb. 12:23, NKJV). It will be presented as glorious (Eph. 5:27), and is the bride of Christ (Rev. 21:9). Since the church is the body of Christ, who is the head of it, God's glory in the church is evidenced by the way the church glorifies Jesus. The weightiness of this responsibility is just one of the many reasons why we need to daily intercede for our churches to be dependent upon and fueled by the strength of the Holy Spirit.

Make your face shine on your servant, and teach me your statutes.

What is the time stamp Paul put on God receiving glory?

What does this teach you about God's purpose for your life? For your church?

How interesting for Paul to intentionally declare that God will be glorified throughout all generations, forever and ever. This part of Paul's prayer echoes an earlier statement he made in his letter, when he said the reason for our eternity in heaven is to ". . . display the immeasurable riches of his grace through his kindness to us in Christ Jesus" (Eph. 2:7). Our salvation brings God glory and is a forever testimony of His love and grace.

Almost like an answer to the generations of hostility where God was not glorified, Paul prayed for His glory to be for all generations. Then he added *forever and ever* (v. 21). Not only will Jesus be glorified through the church here on earth, but He'll be glorified through the church in eternity. All the division from the past is no match for the unity we'll have for eternity. The church has a responsibility to live in harmony and call out sin. We have to be humble and passionately pursue holiness.

Our salvation brings God glory and is a forever testimony of His love and grace.

The church is missing so many opportunities to glorify Jesus today. We are hoarders of grace. We want all that God can give us, but we are selective in how we share it. We've equated following Jesus with making the correct choices regarding political positions and social issues. Instead of unity, which requires understanding someone or something different from us, we're comfortable with division. The church today has spent so much energy on non-critical doctrine that the watching world can't possibly figure out what we believe or what's important. I believe many of the tensions have been simmering beneath the surface for years. The mix of extended periods of isolation, the false courage found in digital communication, the intentional ignorance and insensitivity to the hurts of others, and our overestimated spiritual maturity has created a horrible exposure.

What is one way you've recently seen this tension play out between the church's calling and cultural pressures?

What percentage of your prayers would you estimate are for your church and its leaders compared with prayers for yourself or your family?

In Revelation 2:1-5, we read some of Jesus's own words for the church at Ephesus. He said:

Write to the angel of the church in Ephesus: Thus says the one who holds the seven stars in his right hand and who walks among the seven golden lampstands: I know your works, your labor, and your endurance, and that you cannot tolerate evil people. You have tested those who call themselves apostles and are not, and you have found them to be liars. I know that you have persevered and endured hardships for the sake of my name, and you have not grown weary. But I have this against you: You have abandoned the love you had at first. Remember then how far you have fallen; repent, and do the works you did at first. Otherwise, I will come to you and remove your lampstand from its place, unless you repent.

In the passage you just read, <u>underline</u> what Jesus affirmed about the church in Ephesus. Then, put [brackets] around what He challenged.

If the Ephesians, who received so much guidance and wisdom from Paul, could still stray from glorifying Jesus, how much more might the church today? We are witnesses that this church had sound doctrine, a faithful pastor, and a clear picture of their mission. But they still abandoned their love for Jesus. There are many churches on mission and glorifying Christ in their love, but there are many who are not. One of the responsibilities of every follower of Christ is to pray for a miraculous display of God's power in and through the local and global church.

BEFORE YOU WRAP UP THIS WEEK'S STUDY, LOOK UP THE FOLLOWING VERSES and write the main idea of Paul's prayer in each passage.

Romans 15:5-6	
Ephesians 1:15-21	
Philippians 1:3-5	
Colossians 1:9-21	

What stands out to you from Paul's examples of intercessory prayer?

Remember that we serve a perfect God who gives perfect purpose to imperfect people.

The doxology at the end of Paul's prayer reminds us that when we pray, it is to a God who is abundant—abundant in His love, glory, grace, provision, power, and on and on. Time and again throughout his letters, Paul showed us the importance of intercessory prayer as a way we advocate for others before God and a way we advocate for the lavishness and love of God to show up through us and our churches. It's time to take seriously the call to glorify Jesus through the church, and being an advocate in prayer is a critical way we do that. Remember that we serve a perfect God who gives perfect purpose to imperfect people—to the glory of Jesus Christ, forever, amen.

When You Pray Today

With Paul's example in mind, list a few prayers you should regularly be praying for:

Your church and its leaders—

Other Christians—

Non-Christians—

Make a copy of this list or take a photo of it and keep it somewhere you'll see it often.

WATCH

SESSION SIX

Watch the Session Six video and take notes below.

TO ACCESS THE VIDEO SESSIONS, USE THE INSTRUCTIONS
IN THE BACK OF YOUR BIBLE STUDY BOOK.

170

Discuss

If you are part of a *When You Pray* Bible study group, use this page to take notes during your group time and to keep a record of prayer requests that are mentioned.

May They Be One

BY KRISTI McLELLAND

For our final week together, we will study a powerful and intentional prayer from Jesus. How fitting that a study on what we learn about prayer from the Bible is bookended by the words of our Savior.

This prayer is located in John 17:20-21, and it reads:

I pray not only for these, but also for those who believe in me through their word. May they all be one, as you, Father, are in me and I am in you. May they also be in us, so that the world may believe you sent me.

This Week's Prayer

BIBLE PASSAGE
John 13–17

PRAYER TYPE
Prayers that Unify

Prayer is an overflow of the heart—words given to the living God in faith that He will hear and He will see it through. I've always loved this prayer from John 17 because Jesus mentioned you and me in this moment. We are the later generations of the church, those "who will believe in [Jesus] through [the disciples'] message" (NIV). When Jesus prayed these words two thousand years ago, He had you and me on His mind and heart and in His words prayed to His Father.

For us to better understand this prayer of Jesus, it's important to remember that it didn't just happen out of nowhere. It was a prayer prayed at the end of the most famous meal during Jesus's earthly life and ministry—the Last Supper.

The whole story of the Last Supper is covered in five chapters: John 13–17, a section of John's Gospel referred to as the Upper Room Discourse. We'll spend our five study days together considering some of the key words Jesus gave His disciples during this final meal and ending with His words given to His Father in prayer. Each day we'll study—or as I like to say *feast*, because we don't so much read the Word of God as eat it, take it in, let it do its work in us—a chapter at a time leading into John 17 and the prayer Jesus offered on our behalf. Let's begin our feast.

I pray not only for these, but also for those who believe in me through their word. May they all be one, as you, Father, are in me and I am in you. May they also be in us, so that the world may believe you sent me.

JOHN 17:20-21

DAY ONE

THE LAST SUPPER: WORDS AT A TABLE

Before the Passover Festival, Jesus knew that his hour had come to depart from this world to the Father. Having loved his own who were in the world, he loved them to the end. Now when it was time for supper . . .

JOHN 13:1-2a

TO BEGIN, READ JOHN 13–17.

I'm an only child and highly imaginative. My imagination runs circles around most people, and it's served me well in my Bible reading and understanding. I'm also a visual, experiential learner. I learn best by what I see and what I touch rather than what I hear. When I read the Bible, I envision it. I see it. I imagine what it would have been like to be there, to be in those biblical stories and to witness them with my five senses.

When I had the opportunity to study the Bible in Egypt and Israel in 2007, it significantly fattened my love for the written Word of God. I learned to read the Bible anchored in its historical, cultural, linguistic, and geographical context. I sat in the very places where biblical events took place. I saw it for myself. I love to tell people that I went to Israel and learned the living God is better than I ever knew. The Bible is a living and breathing story, and my hope is to bring it alive for you as you study this week. The Last Supper begins in John 13, so that's where we begin, too. The Bible gives us important behind-the-scenes information from the start.

> **READ JOHN 13:1.** List everything you learn about this moment in Jesus's life from this one verse.

Jesus knew this was the last meal He would share with His disciples before calm was thrown into chaos. He knew the "hour had come," a reference to the crucifixion (v. 1). Can you imagine how Jesus felt during this last meal? Can you imagine all that was moving and stirring in His heart as He ate with His disciples, this group of men He loved so deeply, one last time before everything changed forever?

> Close your eyes and visualize yourself in that scene, at that table. Imagine what it might have been like to recline at the table with Jesus that day.

One of my favorite lines in the whole Bible is found in **JOHN 13:1,**

Having loved his own who were in the world, he loved them to the end.

How did Jesus love His disciples during this last supper? He showered and bathed them with His actions (like washing their feet) and especially with His words. The words He spoke around that table, which are preserved for us in John 13–17, were some of His last words for His disciples then and now, and He knew it.

> *Words of truth.*
>
> *Words of life.*
>
> *Words of encouragement.*
>
> *Words of instruction.*
>
> *Words to explain what was coming next.*
>
> *Words of hope.*
>
> *Words of comfort.*
>
> *Words of vision.*
>
> *Words of purpose.*
>
> *Words of unity binding them together.*
>
> *And words of prayer offered on their behalf (and ours).*

> **READ JOHN 13:2-20.** Summarize the words of Jesus, supported by His actions, at this point in their meal.

Jesus began the Last Supper by washing the feet of His disciples and explaining His action. The looming crucifixion was the ultimate act of sacrificial love—Creator God sacrificing His Son out of love for His creation. With the words in John 13:14-17, Jesus explained that as His disciples, sacrificial servant love would be expected of them, too.

NOW READ JOHN 13:21-30.

A lot is going on in this scene, but I want us to focus on the picture we get of the table. In Jesus's Jewish world two thousand years ago, table fellowship was incredibly important and intimate. Sharing a meal with people meant you welcomed, embraced, and accepted them. The table was the place to recline, to linger, to breathe together, to tell stories; it was the place to share in the comfort of food and fellowship. Middle Eastern meals are lengthy to this very day. Meals I've shared in Israel, Jordan, and Egypt take a long, long time. I learned quickly to never plan something following a meal because the meal itself will take all night!

I've provided a sketch to show you what a typical meal would have looked like in Jesus's world, and it helps us envision the Last Supper with Jesus and His disciples.

Study the sketch and then answer the following questions:

What sticks out to you?

How do you think you would feel experiencing a meal like this?

What would be the mood or personality of a meal like this?

How is it similar to meals as we know them today?

How is it different from meals as we know them today?

As you can see from the picture on the previous page, Jesus and the disciples most likely reclined on the floor, leaning on their left elbows with a pallet of food and drink in front of them to share. Your right hand served as your fork. Seeing this sketch helps us better understand Jesus's exchange with John after Jesus announced someone present at the meal was about to betray Him.

> One of his disciples, the one Jesus loved, was reclining close beside Jesus. Simon Peter motioned to him to find out who it was he was talking about. So he leaned back against Jesus and asked him, "Lord, who is it?"
> JOHN 13:23-25

The sketch shows us how John would have simply leaned back against Jesus to ask this question. Here we see the casual, friendly, warm, open, and lingering feel of an ancient Middle Eastern meal. This was the perfect environment for Jesus's final teaching to His disciples. He knew every minute and every word counted.

READ JOHN 13:31-35 as you wrap up today's study.

Summarize Jesus's words in verses 31-33 in one phrase:

Summarize Jesus's words in verses 34-35 in one phrase:

Jesus intentionally fed His disciples to the full with words that would ring in their heads and hearts for the rest of their lives. I imagine the disciples years later, sitting around fires or reclining at meals, remembering and sharing these words of Jesus—words of encouragement about His divine purpose and a reminder of the call to love others with the sacrificial, selfless love of Jesus.

When You Pray Today

Before you pray, imagine your own "last supper." Think through the following questions and then end with your prayer:

- If you knew you had one meal to share before the end of your life, whom would you invite?

- Where would you host your final meal?

- What food and drink would you serve at your final meal?

- What would you say at your final meal?

- What would you want to include in your final prayer at the end of your final meal?

DAY TWO

THE LAST SUPPER: THE FATHER'S HOUSE

Don't let your heart be troubled.
Believe in God; believe also in me.

JOHN 14:1

Yesterday, we were introduced to the historical, cultural context of the famous Last Supper with Jesus and the disciples in John 13. In John 17, Jesus would end that intimate, intentional, word-filled meal with a strong and mighty prayer on behalf of those disciples and on behalf of us now. My heart feels both comfort and courage when I think about Jesus praying for me, for you, for us all during His final moments on earth.

We pick up the story line of the Last Supper today in John 14. The words of Jesus spoken at this final meal were the last words deposited into His disciples before calm moved to chaos. Like a bank account, He kept adding and adding, speaking and speaking kingdom-rich goodness and hopefulness into them throughout that final meal in order to prepare them for what was to come. His encouragement would conclude with His prayer: "may they all be one, as you, Father, are in me and I am in you" (John 17:21).

Jesus's words during the Last Supper take on extra meaning when we remember that He knew what was coming next.

During the session on prayers of lament, we reflected on how suffering often draws us to the Lord in prayer. Years ago, I served in women's ministry at my church alongside a strong, mature woman of God whose witness I got to watch every day. During our time serving together, we found out she had breast cancer. I remember the day she called to tell me her doctor declared her cancer free. We celebrated and thanked God as a church community on behalf of our church mother and friend. Two years later we found out her cancer had returned—this time in her brain. Along the way we found out that her diagnosis was terminal; she wasn't going to survive it this time. She had a husband, four children, grandchildren, siblings, and on and on. Not to mention a church family who loved and respected her deeply.

I remember going to my dear friend's house for coffee one morning during that season and braving a question: "What does it feel like to know you're dying?" I'll never forget her answer as she sat across from me at her kitchen table. She told me how grateful she was that she had time to say every single word of love and goodbye to anyone and everyone she wanted to give her words. Knowing the end was coming, she took great care with her words. When I learned she had passed away, my first thought was, *She spent every word she wanted to spend. She said everything she wanted to say before leaving this world.*

I think of that dear friend when I read John 13–17. It's in that same spirit that Jesus deposited those words into His disciples. He took time to say every word He wanted to say.

Before we look at the beginning of John 14, read John 13:33,36-37 for some important context.

> **Jesus knew what He was about to face, but His disciples didn't. Based on Peter's response to Jesus's announcement that He was leaving them, how did the disciples take the news?**

One of the things Jesus wanted His disciples to understand was that His time being physically present with them was coming to an end. I can only imagine how frustrated and fearful they were at the thought that their leader, the One they gave up everything to follow and learn from, was leaving them what seemed to be prematurely. You can almost hear the confusion dripping from Peter's words.

WITH THAT IN MIND, READ JOHN 14:1-7.

Jesus's words at the beginning of John 14 provided a powerful and beautiful image from their everyday lives to show His disciples that their coming pain was temporary. He showed them a glimpse of life past the trauma of crucifixion, resurrection, and the absence of His physical presence among them.

He began by telling them to not let their hearts be troubled, and to believe in God (the Father) and in Him (John 14:1a). The Father/Son imagery in John 14 gave His disciples (and us) massive eternal-perspective hope.

Jesus continued in verses 2-3,

> In my Father's house are many rooms. If it were not so, would I have told
> you that I am going to prepare a place for you? If I go away and prepare a
> place for you, I will come again and take you to myself, so that where I am
> you may be also.
>
> JOHN 14:2-3

READ THE PRINTED TEXT OF JOHN 14:2-3 AGAIN. <u>Underline</u> the
words and phrases that describe Jesus's actions on the disciples'
(your!) behalf.

In your own words, what is the good news of these verses?

Why was it important for Jesus's disciples to know they would be
reunited with Jesus, even if they didn't understand what He meant?

Why is it important for us to know this now?

I don't know about you, but I can endure difficult things much better when I know an
end is coming. When I can see my pain and the things pressing me as temporary, I can
endure with the hopefulness of knowing a time will come when I will be on the other side
of it. I tend to struggle in a much deeper way when my pain or suffering seems like it will
never end. Pain where there may not be an exit ramp. Pain where there's no cure, remedy,
or solution. Pain that might accompany me for my whole life.

READ JOHN 14:2 AGAIN.

The imagery of this verse was reflective of betrothal and marriage customs in Jesus's
Jewish world two thousand years ago. The family structure was patriarchal with

the father (*pater*) as head of the household.[1] The family structure was also *patrilocal*, meaning a new bride would leave her father's household and join her new husband in the house of his father.[2] The Hebrew term is *bet av* or the *father's house.*[3]

A typical custom from that time was that upon betrothal (engagement), a father and son would begin building a new room onto the father's house. This would become the room where the son would bring his new bride home after the wedding ceremony. They would live together as a newly married couple and family within the overarching father's house. When the room was finished, the son could go get his bride and bring her home following the wedding.

> Have you ever thought about Jesus's words and imagery given in John 14 as betrothal/marriage imagery? REREAD JOHN 14:1-7 with this family dynamic (and your place in it) in mind.

Jesus knew that His ascension back to heaven would follow shortly after the crucifixion and resurrection (Acts 1:9-11). He knew His days of physically being present with His disciples were limited. It would be understandable for the disciples to be heartbroken, but Jesus didn't want them to be. He wanted them to know that as He physically went away from them, He and His Father would be actively building rooms onto the heavenly *bet av*, the Father's house, in preparation for their arrival. His separation from them would be temporary. They would never be out of His mind or heart, and in the meantime, He would be with them by His Spirit—the Helper He would send in His name.

This is a beautiful picture for us of eternity, of the prominent place we have among the family of God forever. Can you imagine how hopeful these words, this promise, would have been to the disciples long after Jesus had ascended back into heaven and they had a better understanding of what they bore witness to? They knew that but for a little while they would continue living on, sharing the gospel and sharing in kingdom life together, while the Father and Son were preparing their rooms in the Father's house in heaven.

> How does it change your perspective today to know that you will have a permanent home in the family of God forever?

What are one or two ways this familial aspect of eternity can shape your prayers for others? Your prayers for the church?

When you wonder where the living God is or what He's doing in seasons when you're struggling, you have these words of Jesus to comfort you. God is working even now to add your room onto the Father's house. And one day, Jesus is going to return as a groom coming to get His bride (Rev. 19). He is going to come for you. He is going to carry you into the Father's house where you will dwell with God and the family of God forever in perfect *shalom*.

In the meantime, remember that you are a part of the family of God even today, which unites you to your brothers and sisters in Christ in your church, your community, and around the world. You are not alone in life, and you are not alone in mission. We all have the same Father, and we will dwell in the same house in eternity. Make every effort to live out this oneness now. And no matter what you or your church family are facing today, remember you're headed to the Father's house. Don't let your heart be troubled.

When You Pray Today

Look at your answer to the last question. Take a few minutes now to **practice praying for a handful of believers in your life,** specifically for the ways they are living for Jesus today. Then, **voice a prayer for your church,** specifically that it would be a tangible example of the *bet av*, the Father's house, for the people in your community.

DAY THREE

THE LAST SUPPER: HOPE IN AN ANCIENT VINEYARD

I am the vine; you are the branches. The one who remains in me and I in him produces much fruit, because you can do nothing without me.

JOHN 15:5

We pick up our story line today with John 15, the next chapter in the Upper Room Discourse (John 13–17) of the Last Supper. As we walk through this famous last meal with Jesus and His disciples, we inherit the very words He deposited into them on that special, sacred night before Gethsemane, arrest, trial, crucifixion, and resurrection.

Let's imagine this meal in our minds once again. Jesus and His disciples are reclining around a pallet on the floor. Middle Eastern meals are lengthy, patient, and open. Meals are usually a few hours spent together eating, sharing stories, and enjoying the company. During this particular meal, the disciples asked Jesus lots of questions, and Jesus responded with deeply rich and meaningful words.

This is a typical rabbi-disciple (*talmid*, in Hebrew) interaction.[4] A good disciple in Jesus's world wasn't the one with all the answers but the one with lots of questions. Questions were valued, honored, and welcomed. They raise curiosity and cause one to lean in, listen up, and learn. As a rabbi of Israel and as the Son of God, Jesus loves our questions. Not only can He handle them, but from His interactions in the Gospels we know that He welcomes, values, and honors them. He knows that behind every question is a questioner, one who is leaning into Him to listen and learn.

I hope you've learned through this study that prayer is one of the best ways to ask your questions to the living God. Like you saw in the week on prayers of lament, the book of Psalms is full of people who were asking questions—sometimes hard, direct, and honest questions—to the Lord. If you ever wonder how God really feels about your questions, just look at the volume and vulnerability of the ones He had recorded in the Holy Scriptures!

> Before you begin today's study, pray **PSALM 119:108,**
>
> *LORD, please accept my freewill offerings of praise, and teach me your judgments.*

Prayer isn't about saying what we think the Lord wants to hear from us. Prayer is an honest, intimate, and intentional reaching for the Lord in truth, in reality, in the actuality of our lives as they are. The psalms teach us that if we're going to pray, pray honest. And from the passage of Scripture we'll look at today, we'll see that honest prayers flow out of a deeply rooted connection to our heavenly Father.

BEGIN BY READING ALL OF JOHN 15.

Within John 13–17, chapters 15 and 17 are unique. All of the words in John 15 and almost all of John 17 (with the exception of verse 1a) are Jesus's words. In John 15, Jesus poured encouragement onto the disciples, seeding it into them, filling them to the full with hopeful imagery and metaphor to give them confidence before their world would be turned upside down in just a few short hours.

In John 14, Jesus used the metaphor/imagery of the Father's House (the *bet av*) to give hope to His disciples. At the start of John 15, He pulled another image from their everyday lives to encourage them. I love how Jesus put things on the "bottom shelf" for His disciples. He taught them using average, mundane things out of their everyday lives and world to convey the intricacies of the kingdom of God. Jesus met them right where they were. I love Him for this. He meets you and me right where we are, and He meets us with words—the Word of God.

> NOW READ JOHN 15:1-5 AGAIN, slowly this time, visualizing the imagery of Jesus's words.

In John 15, Jesus painted a picture with His words of an ancient vineyard. When I take teams to Israel, we sit in a vineyard and walk through John 15 together. As we look around, the imagery of the vineyard married to Jesus's words provides a somewhat surprising picture and encouragement for us.

> I am the true vine, and my Father is the gardener. He cuts off
> every branch in me that bears no fruit . . .
>
> JOHN 15:1-2a (NIV)

The living God is the gardener.

Jesus is the true vine.

We are the branches growing off of the true vine.

The Bible was given to us so that we might know who the living God is and what He is like. When Jesus referred to His Father as the gardener, it's important to process what that meant in their Jewish world two thousand years ago. Is He the God who cuts us off when we're struggling? Or is there another way to understand Jesus's words and imagery here?

The word translated "cuts off" or "takes away" in verse 2 is the Greek word *airo*. Traditionally, *airo* has two meanings—to "cut off" or to "lift up."[5] What is possibly the better translation of this word in an ancient Mediterranean vineyard just like the ones Jesus and His disciples would have known two thousand years ago?

Paraphrase John 15:2 where "cuts off" is the translation of *airo*.

Now paraphrase John 15:2 where "lifts up" is the translation of *airo*.

A gardener in Jesus's world would first clear a field of smaller stones, leaving some of the larger stones. He would have built a hedge around his vineyard to enclose it. The hedge was usually made of stones piled up together, and it served as a boundary marker and kept animals out of the vineyard. He might even build a watchtower to watch over the vineyard. This was his livelihood, and he had to protect it.

Vines grew along the ground, not up trellises like we imagine in Napa Valley. The morning dew would threaten to sour the grapes if the vines and their branches were left on the ground. A good gardener would walk through his vineyard, checking on his vines and branches. If he saw a vine struggling along the ground, he would lift up the vine and its branches and place them on a larger stone left in the vineyard.

When I sit with my teams in that vineyard in Israel, we sit among vines that have been lifted up onto rocks with the branches growing off of the main vine. It's a striking image as we read these words from Jesus in John 15. Sitting there, I can't help but wonder if a more culturally accurate way of interpreting the Greek word *airo* is to "lift up" rather than to "cut off."

> I am the true vine, and my Father is the gardener. He [lifts up] every branch in me that bears no fruit . . .
>
> JOHN 15:1-2a (NIV)

Sitting at that final last supper with His disciples, Jesus gave them deeply rich encouragement. He knew struggle was coming, their whole lives would be turned upside down in just a few short hours. They were about to enter the crucible—the suffering and the shaking of all they thought they knew.

How would the living God respond to them in their struggle? Like an ancient gardener in his ancient vineyard, He would lift them up. He would set them on a rock. He would position them to grow in difficult trials and sufferings. He would hear their prayers and respond as the "God of all comfort" (2 Cor. 1:3).

What are some areas of your life where you need the Gardener to lift you up on a rock?

Who is the living God? He is the One who loves your questions. He welcomes your questions and can handle all of you. He receives your questions in your moments and seasons of struggle as you lean into Him and listen for Him. He is the One who sees you in your struggle and lifts you up on a rock. He watches over you. He vigilantly positions you to grow and mature even in your sufferings and difficulties. He is a good Gardener.

What are some of the questions you find yourself asking the living God in this season of your life?

What would it look like for you to spend some intentional time today sitting with your questions?

Write your own psalm to the Lord.

Include in it some of your questions. Get honest.

This psalm is between you and the Lord. You are the only two who will ever see it.

THE LAST SUPPER: THE SPIRIT'S HOVERING & HELP

> Nevertheless, I am telling you the truth. It is for your benefit that I go away, because if I don't go away the Counselor will not come to you. If I go, I will send him to you.
>
> JOHN 16:7

We pick up the story line of the Last Supper today in John 16. Remember, we're laying the groundwork for Jesus's prayer for His disciples then and now, but we aren't there yet. As we begin our time in John 16 today, I want us to first pause and remember everything that Jesus has already said to His disciples during this meal.

> **READ BACK OVER JOHN 13–15.** Don't rush it, and remember to visualize yourself reclining at the table with Jesus.

Jesus used His final meal with His disciples to fill them to the full with hopeful, buoyant, life-strengthening, and faith-establishing truths that they would lean on for decades to come after His physical departure from earth. During that final meal, Jesus knew that Gethsemane, arrest, trial, crucifixion, and resurrection were on the way. But He also saw past all of that to His ascension, His return to heaven to be with His Father, which He knew would leave His followers feeling every single emotion under the sun.

The disciples had only known a world where Jesus was present with them in the flesh. They could see, hear, and touch Him. He was their Lord and Rabbi. He often walked so close to them that the dust of His sandals got all over them. Since being called to follow Him, they had walked with Him, ate with Him, sabbathed with Him, prayed with Him, and ministered with Him. They knew what life was like with Him. What would they do after He ascended back to heaven? How painful would that departure be to their hearts? How disruptive to their lives and their sense of purpose? But how deeply encouraging it would be to know He had resurrected and was going back to the Father with death defeated and eternal life made available to all who would believe by faith!

READ JOHN 16:1-6. What did Jesus say His disciples could expect to happen after He left?

Jesus knew that this final meal was the calm before the chaos, the last few moments of "normal" He had with His disciples. It was about to get hard, really hard. Jesus began John 16 with these words, "I have told you these things to keep you from stumbling" (v. 1). Their faith was about to be tested. Their whole world was about to be thrown into the crucible, the very kind of crucible that would threaten to cause them to fall away.

Who would help them after Jesus ascended?

Where would the divine aid come from in the physical absence of Jesus?

Would they be left on their own to fend for themselves?

Or would the living God provide a helper?

READ JOHN 16:7. What bold promise and future hope did Jesus give His disciples?

Jesus promised that after His physical departure, the "Advocate" would come. *Advocate* comes from the Greek word *parakletos* meaning "counselor or legal assistant," so your translation may also say "Counselor" or "Helper."[6] Who was this Advocate? John 16:13 reveals He is the Holy Spirit.

READ JOHN 16:8-15. List everything Jesus promised the Holy Spirit would do for the followers of Jesus.

Jesus had mentioned the coming of the Holy Spirit earlier in the Last Supper. We didn't get a chance to look at these passages then, so let's read them now.

> And I will ask the Father, and he will give you another Counselor to be
> with you forever. He is the Spirit of truth.
>
> JOHN 14:16-17a

> But the Counselor, the Holy Spirit, whom the Father will send in my
> name, will teach you all things and remind you of everything I have
> told you.
>
> JOHN 14:26

What added insights do these verses give you into the work and purpose of the Holy Spirit in the life of the believer?

Jesus wanted His disciples to know He was not leaving them as orphans. He was not leaving them to fend for themselves. The living God would be faithful to send the Spirit after Jesus's ascension back to heaven. Jesus would remain close to them because the Spirit would come.

One of the first and earliest images given to us in the entire Bible has to do with the Spirit of God. At the very genesis, the Spirit is present, and the imagery is gorgeous.

> In the beginning God created the heavens and the earth. Now the earth
> was formless and empty, darkness covered the surface of the watery
> depths, and the Spirit of God was hovering over the surface of the waters.
>
> GENESIS 1:1-2

The word *spirit* in Hebrew is *ruach* meaning "breath, wind, spirit."[7] At the very beginning of the story of the Bible, the Spirit is not only present; the Spirit is actively doing something. The Spirit is "hovering." This word used elsewhere carries the imagery of an eagle fluttering over its young. It carries not only the imagery of rapid back-and-forth movement but has a nurturing essence while hovering. The Spirit hovers like a mother over her young.

When I think of the Spirit of God, I imagine the hovering mentioned in Genesis 1.

> **When you think of the Spirit of God, what imagery from Scripture comes up for you? If you like to draw, draw your response instead of writing it.**

You might have said the dove descending on Jesus at His baptism, or the tongues of fire from Pentecost. Scripture includes many images to help us understand this invisible Person of the Trinity. From the very beginning of the Bible, we're introduced to the Spirit of God as a vigilant nurturer, helper, and comforter. This same Spirit of God present at the beginning of the Bible is the Spirit of God that Jesus keeps referencing during the Last Supper.

For a group of disciples who would soon experience Gethsemane, arrest, trial, crucifixion, resurrection, and ascension, this was very good news! The coming Holy Spirit would lead and guide them into all truth. And the Spirit would help them, comfort them, and nurture them along the path as they walked the path of Jesus in the world.

The Spirit of God even helps us in our prayer life, which is great news after everything we've learned about prayer through our study. Have you ever been so distraught, undone, angry, lost, or sad that you didn't know what to pray? I have absolutely known those times in my life. I have known times when my grief was too great, my pain too heavy, my heart just too undone to even find my words to offer the living God.

> **Have you experienced moments when you did not know how to pray? What is our hope in those moments?**

Our hope is that we are not alone: the Spirit of God is present and ready to help us in prayer.

READ ROMANS 8:26. How does it make you feel to know that the Spirit of God intercedes for you when you don't have the words to give Him?

Think about a time when you sensed the Spirit of God groaning for you when you did not have the words to pray. What stands out as you reflect on that time?

When I think of the Spirit of God, I envision the Spirit hovering. I think back to that first, ancient imagery in Genesis 1 and I feel soothed, encouraged, and even ignited. With the Spirit of God dwelling inside of me, hovering over me, interceding for me with wordless groans, leading and guiding me into all truth and bringing to remembrance the things the Lord has already taught me, I feel more confident living forward.

One of my favorite photos ever taken while in Israel was this photo of a dove hovering over the Jordan River. We were in the middle of baptisms at the Jordan when this dove started flying over us. It was so beautiful! It reminds me always of the Spirit hovering over creation in Genesis 1 and over Jesus at His baptism (Matt. 3:16).

Jesus knew that soon He would no longer be present with them in body but would continue His ministry by His personal presence in the Spirit. Jesus knew that both the Word of God and the Spirit of God would work powerfully in their lives as they carried on His ministry and as the church grew. The faithfulness of the living God would be with them to the end.

> I have told you these things so that in me you may have peace. You will
>
> have suffering in this world. Be courageous! I have conquered the world.

JOHN 16:33

When You Pray Today

Set a ten-minute timer and sit in silence before the Lord. Practice listening to Him and simply **resting in His presence**.

THE LAST SUPPER: EDEN'S *SHALOM* IN UNITY

After Jesus said this, he looked toward heaven and prayed.

JOHN 17:1 (NIV)

We finally made it to John 17 and to the prayer of emphasis for this week. Just as we began by looking at Jesus's model prayer from Matthew 6, we end with another example He gives us of what to say when we pray. John 17 marks the end of the famous Last Supper, and at the start of John 18 we see Jesus headed off to the garden of Gethsemane. After pouring words of truth and encouragement into His disciples, Jesus ended the meal with a lengthy prayer. I love that Jesus not only took time to give a lot of words to His disciples; He gave a lot of words to His Father, too.

> **READ JOHN 17:1-5,** the beginning of Jesus's prayer.
>
> **What is the main point of Jesus's prayer for Himself in these verses?**
>
> **Write down two things you learn about how to pray from Jesus's example in verses 1-5.**

Almost all of John 17 (with the exception of verse 1a) are words prayed by Jesus to the Father on behalf of Himself and His followers. The meal was over, and He had said everything He wanted to say to His disciples. In mere moments they would get up from their Middle Eastern pallet and make their way to Gethsemane.

Knowing that Gethsemane, arrest, trial, crucifixion, resurrection, and ascension awaited Him, Jesus prayed. And it was a powerful and intentional prayer. Jesus began this prayer much like He began His model prayer, by acknowledging the glory of God the Father. He also reminded His followers of His purpose in coming to earth in the first place—to unite people to God, a righting of the wrong done in the garden of Eden. This is the work, the mission, Jesus would command the disciples to join Him in (Matt. 28:19-20).

After praying for Himself, Jesus transitioned to a prayer of petition on behalf of His disciples. How would His followers survive the days, weeks, months, and years to come? How would they live forward in a world without the everyday, physical presence of Jesus in their lives? Jesus prayed the answer.

> READ JOHN 17:6-11. Summarize the main point of this part of Jesus's prayer. (Hint: Pay attention to verse 11.)

The most important prayer Jesus had for His disciples in this critical moment was that they would be one, that they would be unified.

Unity is what I call an "edenic quality." It existed in the garden of Eden long before sin entered the world. In Eden, everything worked and worked together beautifully. Everything functioned in unison with everything else. Peace was the atmosphere of the original garden. In Hebrew the term for this kind of peace is *shalom*, and it was the hallmark feature of the garden.[8] Hebraic *shalom* is about so much more than peace, though. It communicates the idea of wholeness, flourishing, delight, and harmony.

> Knowing what you do about the events that followed Jesus's prayer in John 17, why was a prayer for oneness the exact right thing for Jesus to pray for His disciples? Skim the chapters of John that follow to help you answer.

Jesus knew that the coming events would shake the disciples to their core and shatter their immediate sense of *shalom* in the world. Even the ascension— with the resurrected, victorious Jesus going back to heaven to be with His

The most important prayer Jesus had for His disciples in this critical moment was that they would be one, that they would be unified.

Father—would have felt like such a deep loss to them, as we considered yesterday. Jesus knew they would need each other more than ever in the years to come. And they would not only need each other, they would be strong, healthy, and unified in their gospel mission. Jesus wasn't really leaving them; He would be with them in Spirit, and He had a life-saving job for them to do.

It moves me deeply to read these words by Jesus and to see Jesus contending for them in prayer. He was digging deep by praying something for them, over them, and into them that went all the way back to Eden and extends all the way forward to Revelation 19–22— oneness and unity. This is a story that began in the garden and ends in the garden-city.

Reflect on some of your favorite memories of unity and oneness in Christian community. What made that community such a blessing in your life?

We've studied two images Jesus used as part of His Last Supper teaching. Next to each one, write your thoughts on what that imagery teaches you about the relationship Jesus desires for you to have with other believers.

The Father's House (John 14:2-3)

The Vineyard (John 15:1-8)

NOW READ JOHN 17:20-23. Whom did Jesus have in mind in verses 20-21?

From this prayer, what is the reason why unity with God and with others is so important?

This part of Jesus's prayer honestly brings me to tears. Jesus's prayer for His disciples includes a prayer for you and for me! And He prays the same thing for us that He prayed for His immediate disciples who were physically present with Him in the world.

I pray not only for these, but also for those who believe in me through their word. May they all be one, as you, Father, are in me and I am in you. May they also be in us, so that the world may believe you sent me.
JOHN 17:20-21a

This is Jesus, the Son of God, praying for *YOU* and *ME* in the Bible! On that special night, the very night of the famous Last Supper, Jesus was thinking about us, about all of the people who would believe in Him because of the faithfulness of His disciples and the faithfulness of God to answer this prayer.

The Bible is living and active (Heb. 4:12). It's a story we are being invited into. We don't just learn the story of the Bible. We learn to take our place in it. We cannot make it alone. We were never meant to walk through this life alone. We are meant to live in meaningful, unified harmony with one another. And when we do, it gives the world a clear picture of the love and grace of our Lord (John 17:23). Let me leave you with a story to show you what I mean.

I have had the privilege of being part of a kingdom-oriented community of believers for over twenty years. We are unified in our diversity. Our diversity sharpens us. Our unity strengthens us. I had the opportunity to take my community, my "tribe" as I call them, to Israel in October 2019. We spent fourteen days studying the Bible in the Holy Land together. It was an unreal experience. We laughed so hard. We ate so much food while telling stories every night. We were full of wonder, gratitude, and joy. It felt like a pilgrimage gift the Lord wanted to give each of us and yet a gift to the community as a whole.

Little did we know that we would head home from Israel and into the most difficult year in our community's history together. Three weeks after we returned home, a family suddenly lost their twenty-one-year-old son. It shattered us. We came home from Israel and entered the agony together. I have never known such joy and such pain so close together like that.

A few weeks after the home going service for that young man, we found out that a nineteen-year-old son in another family had leukemia. COVID-19 hit the United States in March 2020 right at the same time the young man went to Vanderbilt University Medical Center for treatment. No one could enter the hospital due to COVID-19 restrictions, so groups of us would sit outside their window in the hospital courtyard. We just kept coming to be present, to pray, to bring food, to be a comfort as our friends looked out their hospital window to see that we were still there. We were sitting in that same courtyard the morning he passed away.

Two sons lost within six months of each other. Joy turned to unimaginable pain. It was another round of prayers, visits with food, homegoing service preparations, checking on each other even while none of us were even remotely OK. We were one in our joy while in Israel. We were one in the agony of that year and the prolonged sense of deep loss since that year.

> **What are some of the hardest things you have walked through with community?**

> **What did you learn about the unity of the body of Christ through that crucible you endured? What did you learn about the power and importance of prayer?**

Oneness is the way of the kingdom of God in the world. Gospel-centered, kingdom-oriented unity has always been a unity within diversity. Unity does not occur when we become the same. True, robust, healthy and vibrant unity happens within our unique and diverse expressions. The church is best expressed as a bouquet of unique flowers rather than twelve red roses. We are better together.

Jesus prayed we would be one. Let's do all we can to honor Him as followers of Jesus seeking oneness, unity, harmony, wholeness, flourishing, and delight. I pray our oneness and unity will give the world an ancient taste of Eden and a future taste of the new heaven and new earth fully realized.

How delightfully good when brothers live together in harmony! It is like fine oil on the head, running down on the beard, running down Aaron's beard onto his robes. It is like the dew of Hermon falling on the mountains of Zion. For there the Lord has appointed the blessing—life forevermore.

PSALM 133

How can you seek to cultivate a sense of oneness within your family, church, and community? What role can prayer play? Reflect on what you've learned about prayer from our study.

Write down two takeaways you have about prayer from Jesus's prayer in John 17.

1.

2.

When You Pray Today

Read back over the two takeaways you recorded at the end of today's study. Use both of those as points of emphasis as you spend time now with the Lord in prayer.

WATCH

SESSION SEVEN

Watch the Session Seven video and take notes below.

TO ACCESS THE VIDEO SESSIONS, USE THE INSTRUCTIONS
IN THE BACK OF YOUR BIBLE STUDY BOOK.

Discuss

If you are part of a *When You Pray* Bible study group, use this page to take notes during your group time and to keep a record of prayer requests that are mentioned.

ENDNOTES

Session Two

1. Darrell L. Bock, *Luke: 9:51–24:53*, vol. 2, Baker Exegetical Commentary on the New Testament (Grand Rapids, MI: Baker Academic, 1996).
2. R. T. France, *The Gospel of Matthew*, The New International Commentary on the New Testament (Grand Rapids, MI: Wm. B. Eerdmans Publication Co., 2007), 239.
3. Kelly Minter, *The Blessed Life: A 90-Day Devotional through the Teachings and Miracles of Jesus* (Nashville, B&H Books, 2023), 124.
4. Ibid., 88.
5. Craig Blomberg, *Matthew*, vol. 22, The New American Commentary (Nashville: Broadman & Holman Publishers, 1992), 119.
6. Jonathan T. Pennington, *The Sermon on the Mount and Human Flourishing* (Grand Rapids, MI: Baker Publishing Group, 2017), 233.
7. Blomberg, 119.
8. Pennington, 100.
9. Dallas Willard, *The Divine Conspiracy* (HarperCollins e-Books), 399.
10. Minter, *The Blessed Life,* 12.
11. Scot McKnight, *Sermon on the Mount*, ed. Tremper Longman III, *The Story of God Bible Commentary* (Grand Rapids, MI: Zondervan, 2013), 180.
12. Ibid.
13. Kelly Minter, *Encountering God* (Nashville, Lifeway Press, 2021), 56.
14. John R. W. Stott, *The Message of the Sermon on the Mount (Matthew 5-7): Christian Counter-Culture*, The Bible Speaks Today (Leicester; Downers Grove, IL: InterVarsity Press, 1985), 148.
15. Ibid., 148–149.
16. Minter, *Encountering God*, 59.
17. "G1689 - *emblepō* - Strong's Greek Lexicon," Blue Letter Bible, https://www.blueletterbible.org/lexicon/g1689/nasb20/mgnt/0-1/
18. "G2648 - *katamanthanō* - Strong's Greek Letter Bible, https://www.blueletterbible.org/lexicon/g2648/kjv/tr/0-1/
19. Stott, 149.
20. Daniel L. Akin, *1, 2, 3 John*, vol. 38, The New American Commentary (Nashville: Broadman & Holman Publishers, 2001), 84.
21. C. S. Lewis, letter to Phoebe Hesketh (W), Cambridge, June 14, 1960, in *The Collected Letters of C. S. Lewis*, vol. 3 (New York: HarperCollins, 2007), 1,162.
22. John Stott, *Sermon on the Mount: Seeking First the Kingdom of God: 13 Studies for Individuals or Groups*, LifeGuide Bible Study (InterVarsity Press, 1987), 73.
23. Minter, *Encountering God*, 61.
24. Ibid.
25. Pennington, 227.
26. Leon Morris, *The Gospel according to Matthew, The Pillar New Testament Commentary* (Grand Rapids, MI; Leicester, England: W.B. Eerdmans; Inter-Varsity Press, 1992), 73.
27. Minter, *The Blessed Life,* 95.

Session Three

1. Brett Scott Provance, *Pocket Dictionary of Liturgy & Worship* (Downers Grove, IL: InterVarsity Press, 2009), 102.
2. Matthew 6:9.
3. Michael Green, *The Message of Matthew: The Kingdom of Heaven*, The Bible Speaks Today (Leicester, England; Downers Grove, IL: InterVarsity Press, 2001), 106.
4. D. A. Carson, *Matthew*, The Expositor's Bible Commentary: Matthew, Mark, Luke, ed. Frank E. Gaebelein, vol. 8 (Grand Rapids, MI: Zondervan Publishing House, 1984), 187.
5. Sarah Hinlicky Wilson, "Blessed Are the Barren," *Christianity Today*, December, 2007, https://www.christianitytoday.com/ct/2007/december/21.22.html.
6. Robert D. Bergen, *1, 2 Samuel*, vol. 7, The New American Commentary (Nashville: Broadman & Holman Publishers, 1996), 62.
7. Spiros Zodhiates, *The Complete Word Study Dictionary: New Testament* (Chattanooga, TN: AMG Publishers, 2000).
8. Joyce G. Baldwin, *1 and 2 Samuel: An Introduction and Commentary*, vol. 8, Tyndale Old Testament Commentaries (Downers Grove, IL: InterVarsity Press, 1988), 56.
9. Bergen, 1, 2 Samuel, 66.
10. Alexander Maclaren, *The Gospel According to Saint Luke*, Exposition of Holy Scripture (New York: A. C. Armstrong and Son, 1909), 134.
11. Dan Allender, *The Cry of the Soul* (Colorado Springs: NavPress, 1994).
12. Rick Stedman, *Praying the Psalms* (Eugene: Harvest House Publishers, 2016), 146.
13. Joyce G. Baldwin, *1 and 2 Samuel: An Introduction and Commentary*, 56.
14. "H519 - *'āmâ* - Strong's Hebrew Lexicon," Blue Letter Bible, https://www.blueletterbible.org/lexicon/h519/kjv/wlc/0-1/.
15. Bergen, 72–73.
16. Ibid., 76–77.

Session Four

1. John Calvin, *Institutes of the Christian Religion*, vol. 1, ed. Henry Beveridge (Edinburgh: The Calvin Translation Society, 1845), 47.
2. A. W. Tozer, *The Knowledge of the Holy* (New York: Harper Collins, 1978), 49.
3. Ibid., 34.
4. Ibid., 67.
5. Ibid., 22.
6. C. H. Spurgeon, Sermon on Malachi 3:6, delivered January 7, 1855 at New Park Street Chapel, Southwark, https://answersingenesis.org/education/spurgeon-sermons/1-the-immutability-of-god/.

Session Five

1. John Calvin, *Commentary on the Book of Psalms*, vol. 1 (Edinburgh: The Calvin Translation Society, 1845), 181.
2. "What are the psalms of lament?," Got Questions, https://www.gotquestions.org/psalms-of-lament.html.
3. Ibid.
4. Laura McHale, *Neuroscience for Organizational Communication* (Singapore: Springer Nature Singapore Pte Ltd., 2022), 69–70.

Session Six

1. Provance, *Pocket Dictionary of Liturgy & Worship*, 102.
2. "G3965 - *patria* - Strong's Greek Lexicon," Blue Letter Bible, https://www.blueletterbible.org/lexicon/g3965/kjv/tr/0-1/.
3. "The History of the Fire Hydrant," Inspect Point, https://www.inspectpoint.com/fire-hydrant/.
4. "Ephesians 3:16," BibleHub, https://biblehub.com/commentaries/ephesians/3-16.htm.
5. Strong's G2730, Precept Austin, https://www.preceptaustin.org/ephesians_316-17.
6. "Ephesians 3:16-17 Commentary," Precept Austin, February 2, 2019, https://www.preceptaustin.org/ephesians_316-17.
7. Kenneth S. Wuest, *Wuest's Word Studies* (Grand Rapids, MI: Wm. B. Eerdmans Publishing Company, 2002), 91.
8. Steve Cole, sermon on Ephesians, delivered 2007–2008 at Flagstaff Christian Fellowship, Flagstaff, AZ, https://bible.org/book/export/html/22010.

Session Seven

1. "G3962 - *patēr* - Strong's Greek Lexicon," Blue Letter Bible, https://www.blueletterbible.org/lexicon/g3962/kjv/tr/0-1/.
2. Philip J. King and Lawrence E. Stager, *Life in Biblical Israel* (Louisville, KY: Westminster John Knox Press, 2001), 38.
3. John Rogerson and Philip R. Davies, *The Old Testament World* (London: T&T Clark International, 2005), 32.
4. "H8527 - *talmîd* - Strong's Hebrew Lexicon," Blue Letter Bible, https://www.blueletterbible.org/lexicon/h8527/kjv/wlc/0-1/.
5. "G142 - *airō* - Strong's Greek Lexicon," Blue Letter Bible, https://www.blueletterbible.org/lexicon/g142/kjv/tr/0-1/.
6. "G3875 - *paraklētos* - Strong's Greek Lexicon," Blue Letter Bible, https://www.blueletterbible.org/lexicon/g3875/kjv/tr/0-1/.
7. "H7307 - *rûah* - Strong's Hebrew Lexicon," Blue Letter Bible, https://www.blueletterbible.org/lexicon/h7307/kjv/wlc/0-1/.
8. "H7965 - *šālôm* - Strong's Hebrew Lexicon," Blue Letter Bible, https://www.blueletterbible.org/lexicon/h7965/kjv/wlc/0-1/.

LET'S BE FRIENDS!

BLOG

We're here to help you grow in your faith, develop as a leader, and find encouragement as you go.

lifewaywomen.com

SOCIAL

Find inspiration in the in-between moments of life.

@lifeaywomen

NEWSLETTER

Be the first to hear about new studies, events, giveaways, and more by signing up.

lifeway.com/womensnews

APP

Download the Lifeway Women app for Bible study plans, online study groups, a prayer wall, and more!

 Google Play App Store

Lifeway women

Looking for more?
Check out these resources
by the *When You Pray* authors!

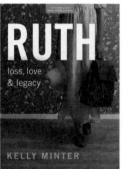

RUTH
By Kelly Minter

Understand how God proves Himself to be the faithful One who rescues, revives, and restores as you study the book of Ruth.
(7 sessions)

lifeway.com/ruth

AMOS
By Jennifer Rothschild

Be challenged to "seek God and live" as you study Amos's prophecy offering an invitation to a transformative and fulfilling life that brings peace to ourselves and those around us. (8 sessions)

lifeway.com/amos

JUDE
By Jackie Hill Perry

Dive into themes of being called, loved, and kept, and learn how to point others to Jesus in grace and truth as you study the book of Jude.
(7 sessions)

lifeway.com/jude

WORLD ON FIRE (B&H)
By Jada Edwards and more

Explore some of the polarizing issues of our day and how the unexpected wisdom of Jesus can help us be more discerning and Christlike amidst them.

lifeway.com/jadaedwards

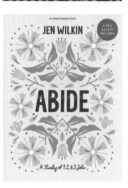

ABIDE
By Jen Wilkin

Discover how we can hold on to assurance of our faith, discern the truth from a lie, and know God loves us through the letters of 1, 2, and 3 John. (10 sessions)

lifeway.com/abide

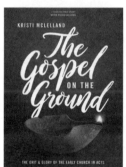

THE GOSPEL ON THE GROUND
By Kristi McLelland

See how God's Word can sustain us even in the most difficult of times and embrace the transformative grace we experience as children of God in His kingdom of celebration.
(7 sessions)

lifeway.com/gospelontheground

To order by phone call 800.458.2772.

Lifeway women

Pricing and availability subject to change without notice.

Get the most from your study.

DVD Set, includes 7 video teaching sessions, each approximately 25–45 minutes

IN THIS STUDY, YOU'LL:

- Explore the different types of prayer modeled in Scripture.
- Understand how prayer unites believers to God and to one another.
- Learn how to overcome struggles that keep you from talking to God.

To enrich your study experience, consider the accompanying *When You Pray* video teaching sessions, approximately 25–45 minutes each, from Kelly Minter, Jackie Hill Perry, Jen Wilkin, Jennifer Rothschild, Jada Edwards, and Kristi McLelland.

STUDYING ON YOUR OWN?

Watch these teaching sessions, available via redemption code for individual video-streaming access, printed in this Bible study book.

LEADING A GROUP?

Each group member will need a *When You Pray* Bible Study Book, which includes video access. Because all participants will have access to the video content, you can choose to watch the videos outside of your group meeting if desired. Or, if you're watching together and someone misses a group meeting, she'll have the flexibility to catch up! A DVD set is also available to purchase separately if desired. You can access the leader guide at lifeway.com/whenyoupray.

Group Experience Box, includes 1 Bible study book, 1 DVD set, 1 Leader Guide, and fun extras, including nametags, Scripture art centerpieces, 1 tassel banner, 1 pack of dual tip pens, 1 tote bag, and 5 *When You Pray* journals

Browse study formats, a free session sample, a leader guide, video clips, church promotional materials, and more at

lifeway.com/whenyoupray

HERE'S YOUR VIDEO ACCESS.

To stream *When You Pray* Bible study video teaching sessions, follow these steps:

1. Go to my.lifeway.com/redeem and register or log in to your Lifeway account.

2. Enter this redemption code to gain access to your individual-use video license:

PDTR3WMSS37S

Once you've entered your personal redemption code, you can stream the video teaching sessions any time from your Digital Media page on my.lifeway.com or watch them via the Lifeway On Demand app on any TV or mobile device via your Lifeway account.

There's no need to enter your code more than once! To watch your streaming videos, just log in to your Lifeway account at my.lifeway.com or watch using the Lifeway On Demand app.

QUESTIONS? WE HAVE ANSWERS!
Visit support.lifeway.com and search "Video Redemption Code" or call our Tech Support Team at 866.627.8553.